ELIZABETHAN ESSAYS

ELIZABETHAN ESSAYS

BY

T. S. ELIOT

HASKELL HOUSE

Publishers of Scholarly Books

NEW YORK

1964

published by

HASKELL HOUSE

Publishers of Scholarly Books

30 East 10th Street • New York, N. Y. 10003

Library of Congress Catalog Card Number: 65-15878

PRINTED IN UNITED STATES OF AMERICA

CONTENTS

FOUR ELIZABETHAN DRAMATISTS   7

CHRISTOPHER MARLOWE   21

SHAKESPEARE AND THE STOICISM OF   33
    SENECA

HAMLET   55

BEN JONSON   65

THOMAS MIDDLETON   87

THOMAS HEYWOOD   101

CYRIL TOURNEUR   117

JOHN FORD   135

PHILIP MASSINGER   153

JOHN MARSTON   177

FOUR ELIZABETHAN DRAMATISTS

A PREFACE TO AN UNWRITTEN BOOK

To attempt to supplement the criticism of Lamb, Coleridge, and Swinburne on these four Elizabethan dramatists—Webster, Tourneur, Middleton, and Chapman—is a task for which I now believe the time has gone by. What I wish to do is to define and illustrate a point of view toward the Elizabethan drama, which is different from that of the nineteenth-century tradition. There are two accepted and apparently opposed critical attitudes toward Elizabethan drama, and what I shall endeavour to show is that these attitudes are identical, and that another attitude is possible. Furthermore, I believe that this alternative critical attitude is not merely a possible difference of personal bias, but that it is the inevitable attitude for our time. The statement and explication of a conviction about such an important body of dramatic literature, toward what is in fact the only distinct form of dramatic literature that England has produced, should be something more than an exercise in mental ingenuity or in refinement of taste: it should be something of revolutionary influence on the future of drama. Contemporary literature, like contemporary politics, is confused by the moment-to-moment struggle for existence; but the time arrives when an examination of principles is necessary. I believe that the theatre has reached a point at which a revolution in principles should take place.

The accepted attitude toward Elizabethan drama was established on the publication of Charles Lamb's *Specimens*. By publishing these selections, Lamb set in motion the enthusiasm for poetic drama which still persists, and at the same time encouraged the formation of a distinction which is, I believe, the ruin of modern drama—the distinction between drama and literature. For the *Specimens* made it possible to read the plays as poetry while neglecting their function on the stage. It is for this reason that all modern opinion of the Elizabethans seems to spring from Lamb, for all modern opinion rests upon the admission that poetry and drama are two separate things, which can only be *combined* by a writer of exceptional genius. The difference between the people who prefer Elizabethan drama, in spite of what they admit to be its dramatic defects, and the people who prefer modern drama although acknowledging that it is never good poetry, is comparatively unimportant. For in either case, you are committed to the opinion that a play can be good literature but a bad play and that it may be a good play and bad literature—or else that it may be outside of literature altogether.

On the one hand we have Swinburne, representative of the opinion that plays exist as literature, and on the other hand Mr. William Archer, who with great lucidity and consistency maintains the view that a play need not be literature at all. No two critics of Elizabethan drama could appear to be more opposed than Swinburne and Mr. William Archer; yet their assumptions are fundamentally the same, for the distinction between poetry and drama, which Mr. Archer makes explicit, is implicit in the view of Swinburne; and Swinburne as well as Mr. Archer allows us to entertain the belief that the difference between modern drama and Elizabethan drama is represented by a gain of dramatic technique and the loss of poetry.

Mr. Archer in his brilliant and stimulating book,[1] succeeded in making quite clear all of the dramatic faults of Elizabethan drama. What vitiates his analysis is his failure to see why these faults are faults, and not simply different conventions. And he gains his apparent victory over the Elizabethans for this reason, that the Elizabethans themselves admit the

[1] *The Old Drama and the New* (Heinemann, 1923).

9

same criteria of realism that Mr. Archer asserts. The great vice of English drama from Kyd to Galsworthy has been that its aim of realism was unlimited. In one play, *Everyman*, and perhaps in that one play only, we have a drama within the limitations of art; since Kyd, since *Arden of Feversham*, since *The Yorkshire Tragedy*, there has been no form to arrest, so to speak, the flow of spirit at any particular point before it expands and ends its course in the desert of exact likeness to the reality which is perceived by the most commonplace mind. Mr. Archer confuses faults with conventions; the Elizabethans committed faults and muddled their conventions. In their plays there are faults of inconsistency, faults of incoherency, faults of taste, there are nearly everywhere faults of carelessness. But their great weakness is the same weakness as that of modern drama, it is the lack of a convention. Mr. Archer facilitates his own task of destruction, and avoids offending popular opinion, by making an exception of Shakespeare; but Shakespeare, like all his contemporaries, was aiming in more than one direction. In a play of Æschylus, we do not find that certain passages are literature and other passages drama; every style of utterance in the play bears a relation to the whole and because of this relation is dramatic in itself. The imitation of life is circumscribed, and the approaches to ordinary speech and withdrawals from ordinary speech are not without relation and effect upon each other. It is essential that a work of art should be self-consistent, that an artist should consciously or unconsciously draw a circle beyond which he does not trespass: on the one hand actual life is always the material, and on the other hand an abstraction from actual life is a necessary condition to the creation of the work of art.

Let us try to conceive how the Elizabethan drama would appear to us if we had in existence what has never existed in the English language: a drama formed within a conventional scheme—the convention of an individual dramatist, or of a number of dramatists working in the same form at the same time. And when I say convention, I do not necessarily mean any particular convention of subject matter, of treatment, of verse or of dramatic form, of general philosophy of life or any other convention which has already been used. It may be some quite new selection or structure or distortion in subject matter or technique; any form or rhythm imposed upon the world of action. We will take the point of view of persons accustomed to this convention and finding the expression of their dramatic impulses in it. From this point of view such performances as were those of the Phoenix Society are most illuminating. For the drama, the existence of which I suppose, will have its special conventions of the stage and the actor as well as of the play itself. An actor in an Elizabethan play is either too realistic or too abstract in his treatment, whatever system of speech, of expression and of movement he adopts. The play is for ever betraying him. An Elizabethan play was in some ways as different from a modern play, its performance is almost as much a lost art, as if it were a drama of Æschylus or Sophocles. And in some ways it is more difficult to reproduce. For it is easier to present the effect of something in a firm convention, than the effect of something which was aiming, blindly enough, at something else. The difficulty in presenting Elizabethan plays is that they are liable to be made too modern, or falsely archaic. Why are the asides ridiculous, which Mr. Archer reprehends in *A Woman Killed with Kindness*? Because they are not a convention, but a subterfuge; it is not Heywood who assumes that asides are inaudible, it is Mrs. Frankford who *pretends* not to hear Wendoll. A convention is not ridiculous: a subterfuge makes us extremely uncomfortable. The weakness of the Elizabethan drama is not its defect of realism, but its attempt at realism; not its conventions, but its lack of conventions.

In order to make an Elizabethan drama give a satisfactory effect as a work of art, we should have to find a method of acting different from that of contemporary social drama, and at the same time to attempt to express all the emotions of actual life in the way in which they actually would be expressed: the result would be something like a performance of *Agamemnon* by the Guitrys. The effect upon actors who attempt to specialize in Shakespearian or other seventeenth-century revivals is unfortunate. The actor is called upon for a great deal that is not his business, and is left to his own devices for things in which he should be trained. His stage personality has to be supplied from and confounded with his real personality. Anyone who has observed one of the great dancers of the Russian school will have observed that the man or the woman whom we admire is a being who exists only during the performances, that it is a personality, a vital flame which appears from nowhere, disappears into nothing and is complete and sufficient in its appearance. It is a conventional being, a being which exists only in and for the work of art which is the ballet. A great actor on the ordinary stage is a person who also exists off it and who supplies the role which he performs with the person which he is. A ballet is apparently a thing which exists only as acted and would appear to be a creation much more of the dancer than of the choreographer. This is not quite true. It is a development of several centuries into a strict form. In the ballet only that is left to the actor which is properly the actor's part. The general movements are set for him. There are only limited movements that he can make, only a limited degree of emotion that he can express. He is not called upon for his personality. The differences between a great dancer and a merely competent dancer is in the vital flame, that impersonal, and, if you like, inhuman force which transpires between each of the great dancer's movements. So it would be in a strict form of drama; but in realistic drama, which is drama striving steadily to escape the conditions of art, the human being intrudes. Without the human being and without this intrusion, the drama cannot be performed, and this is as true of Shakespeare as it is of Henry Arthur Jones. A play of Shakespeare's and a play of Henry Arthur Jones's are essentially of the same type, the difference being that Shakespeare is very much greater and Mr. Jones very much more skilful. They are both dramatists to be read rather than seen, because it is precisely in that drama which depends upon the interpretation of an actor of genius, that we ought to be on our guard against the actor. The difference is, of course, that without the actor of genius the plays of Mr. Jones are nothing and the plays of Shakespeare are still to be read. But a true acting play is surely a play which does not depend upon the actor for anything but acting, in the sense in which a ballet depends upon the dancer for dancing. Lest anyone should fall into a contrary misunderstanding, I will explain that I do not by any means intend the actor to be an automaton, nor would I admit that the human actor can be replaced by a marionette. A great dancer, whose attention is set upon carrying out an appointed task, provides the life of the ballet through his movements; in the same way the drama would depend upon a great trained actor. The advantages of convention for the actor are precisely similar to its advantages for the author. No artist produces great art by a deliberate attempt to express his personality. He expresses his personality indirectly through concentrating upon a task which is a task in the same sense as the making of an efficient engine or the turning of a jug or a table-leg.

The art of the Elizabethans is an impure art. If it be objected that this is a prejudice of the case, I can only reply that one must criticize from some point of view and that it is better to know what one's point of view is. I know that I rebel against most[1] performances of Shakespeare's plays because I want a direct relationship between the work of art and myself, and I want the performance to be such as will not interrupt or alter this relationship any more than it is an alteration or interruption for me to superpose a second inspection of a picture or build-

[1] A really good performance of Shakespeare, such as the very best productions of the Old Vic and Sadler's Wells, may add much to our understanding.

ing upon the first. I object, in other words, to the interpretation, and I would have a work of art such that it needs only to be completed and cannot be altered by each interpretation. Now it is obvious that in realistic drama you become more and more dependent upon the actor. And this is another reason why the drama which Mr. Archer desires, as the photographic and gramophonic record of its time, can never exist. The closer a play is built upon real life, the more the performance by one actor will differ from another, and the more the performances of one generation of actors will differ from those of the next. It is furthermore obvious that what we ask involves a considerable sacrifice of a certain kind of interest. A character in the conventional play can never be as real as is the character in a realistic play while the role is being enacted by a great actor who has made the part his own. I can only say that where-ever you have a form you make some sacrifice against some gain.

If we examine the faults which Mr. Archer finds in Elizabethan drama, it is possible to come to the conclusion (already indicated) that these faults are due to its tendencies rather than what are ordinarily called its conventions. I mean that no single conven-tion of Elizabethan drama, however ridiculous it may be made to appear, is essentially bad. Neither the soliloquy, nor the aside, nor the ghost, nor the blood-

and-thunder, nor absurdity of place or time is in itself absurd. There are, of course, definite faults of bad writing, careless writing, and bad taste. A line-by-line examination of almost any Elizabethan play, including those of Shakespeare, would be a fruitful exercise. But these are not the faults which weaken the foundations. What is fundamentally objectionable is that in the Elizabethan drama there has been no firm principle of what is to be postulated as a convention and what is not. The fault is not with the ghost but with the presentation of a ghost on a plane on which he is inappropriate, and with the confusion between one kind of ghost and another. The three witches in *Macbeth* are a distinguished example of correct supernaturalism amongst a race of ghosts who are too frequently equivocations. It seems to me strictly an error, although an error which is condoned by the success of each passage in itself, that Shakespeare should have introduced into the same play ghosts belonging to such different categories as the three sisters and the ghost of Banquo.[1] The aim of the Elizabethans was to attain complete realism without surrendering any of the advantages which as artists they observed in unrealistic conventions.

We shall take up the work of four Elizabethan

[1] This will appear to be an objection as pedantic as that of Thomas Rymer to *Othello*. But Rymer makes out a very good case.

dramatists and attempt to subject them to an analysis
from the point of view which I have indicated. We
shall take the objections of Mr. Archer to each one
of these dramatists and see if the difficulty does not
reside in this confusion of convention and realism,
and we must make some attempt also to illustrate
the faults as distinguished from the conventions.
There were, of course, tendencies toward form.
There was a general philosophy of life, if it may be
called such, based on Seneca and other influences
which we find in Shakespeare as in the others. It is a
philosophy which, as Mr. Santayana observed in an
essay which passed almost unheeded, may be summarized in the statement that Duncan is in his grave.
Even the philosophical basis, the general attitude
toward life of the Elizabethans, is one of anarchism,
of dissolution, of decay. It is in fact exactly parallel
and indeed one and the same thing with their artistic
greediness, their desire for every sort of effect together, their unwillingness to accept any limitation
and abide by it. The Elizabethans are in fact a part of
the movement of progress or deterioration which
has culminated in Sir Arthur Pinero and in the present regimen of Europe.[1]

[1] Mr. Archer calls it progress. He has certain predispositions.
'Shakespeare', he says, 'was not alive to the great idea which
differentiates the present age from all that have gone before—
the idea of progress.' And he admits, speaking of Elizabethan

The case of John Webster, and in particular *The Duchess of Malfy*, will provide an interesting example of a very great literary and dramatic genius directed toward chaos. The case of Middleton is an interesting one, because we have from the same hand plays so different as *The Changeling, Women Beware Women, The Roaring Girl,* and *A Game at Chess.*[1] In the one great play of Tourneur's, the discord is less apparent, but not less real. Chapman appears to have been potentially perhaps the greatest artist of all these men: his was the mind which was the most classical, his was the drama which is the most independent in its tendency toward a dramatic form— although it may seem the most formless and the most indifferent to dramatic necessities. If we can establish the same consequence independently by an examination of the Elizabethan philosophy, the Elizabethan dramatic form, and the variations in the rhythms of Elizabethan blank verse as employed by several of the greatest dramatists, we may come to conclusions which will enable us to understand why

drama in general, that 'here and there a certain glimmer of humanitarian feeling is perceptible'.

[1] I agree with Mr. Dugdale Sykes, to whose acute observations I am under a great debt, that certain work attributed to Middleton is not Middleton's, but there appears to be no reason for questioning the authorship of the plays I have just mentioned.

Mr. Archer, who is the opponent of the Elizabethans, should also be unconsciously their last
champion, and why he should be a believer in progress, in the growth of humanitarian feeling, and in
the superiority and efficiency of the present age.

CHRISTOPHER MARLOWE

Swinburne observes of Marlowe that 'the father of English tragedy and the creator of English blank verse was therefore also the teacher and the guide of Shakespeare'. In this sentence there are two misleading assumptions and two misleading conclusions. Kyd has as good a title to the first honour as Marlowe; Surrey has a better title to the second; and Shakespeare was not taught or guided by one of his predecessors or contemporaries alone. The less questionable judgment is, that Marlowe exercised a strong influence over later drama, though not himself as great a dramatist as Kyd; that he introduced several new tones into blank verse, and commenced the dissociative process which drew it further and further away from the rhythms of rhymed verse; and that when Shakespeare borrowed from him, which was pretty often at the beginning, Shakespeare either made something inferior or something different.

The comparative study of English versification at various periods is a large tract of unwritten history. To make a study of blank verse alone would be to elicit some curious conclusions. It would show, I believe, that blank verse within Shakespeare's lifetime was more highly developed, that it became the vehicle of more varied and more intense feeling than it has ever conveyed since; and that after the erection of the Chinese Wall of Milton, blank verse has suffered not only arrest but retrogression. That the blank verse of Tennyson, for example, a consummate master of this form in certain applications, is cruder (*not* 'rougher' or less perfect in technique) than that of half a dozen contemporaries of Shakespeare; cruder, because less capable of expressing complicated, subtle, and surprising emotions.

Every writer who has written any blank verse worth saving has produced particular tones which his verse and no other's is capable of rendering; and we should keep this in mind when we talk about 'influences' and 'indebtedness'. Shakespeare is 'universal' because he has more of these tones than anyone else; but they are all out of the one man; one man cannot be more than one man; there might have been six Shakespeares at once without conflicting frontiers; and to say that Shakespeare expressed nearly all human emotions, implying that he left very little for anyone else, is a radical misunderstanding of art and the artist—a misunderstanding which, even when explicitly rejected, may lead to our neglecting the effort of attention necessary to discover the specific properties of the verse of Shakespeare's contemporaries. The development of blank verse may be likened to the analysis of that astonishing industrial product coal-tar. Marlowe's verse is one of the earlier derivatives, but it possesses properties which are not repeated in any of the analytic or synthetic blank verses discovered somewhat later.

The 'vices of style' of Marlowe's and Shakespeare's age is a convenient name for a number of vices, no one of which, perhaps, was shared by all of the writers. It is pertinent, at least, to remark that Marlowe's 'rhetoric' is not, or not characteristically, Shakespeare's rhetoric; that Marlowe's rhetoric consists in a pretty simple huffe-snuffe bombast, while Shakespeare's is more exactly a vice of style, a tortured perverse ingenuity of images which dissipates instead of concentrating the imagination, and which may be due in part to influences by which Marlowe was untouched. Next, we find that Marlowe's vice is one which he was gradually attenuating, and even, what is more miraculous, turning into a virtue. And we find that this poet of torrential imagination recognized many of his best bits (and those of one or two others), saved them, and reproduced them more than once, almost invariably improving them in the process.

It is worth while noticing a few of these versions, because they indicate, somewhat contrary to usual opinion, that Marlowe was a deliberate and conscious workman. Mr. J. M. Robertson has spotted an interesting theft of Marlowe's from Spenser. Here is Spenser (*Faery Queen,* I. vii. 32):

> *Like to an almond tree y-mounted high*
> > *On top of green Selinis all alone,*
> *With blossoms brave bedeckèd daintily;*
> > *Whose tender locks do tremble every one*
> *At every little breath that under heaven is blown.*

And here Marlowe (*Tamburlaine,* Part II, Act IV. Sc. iv):

> *Like to an almond tree y-mounted high*
> *Upon the lofty and celestial mount*
> *Of evergreen Selinus, quaintly deck'd*
> *With blooms more white than Erycina's brows,*
> *Whose tender blossoms tremble every one*
> *At every little breath that thorough heaven is*
> > *blown.*

This is interesting, not only as showing that Marlowe's talent, like that of most poets, was partly synthetic, but also because it seems to give a clue to some particularly 'lyric' effects found in *Tamburlaine,* not in Marlowe's other plays, and not, I believe,

anywhere else. For example, the praise of Zenocrate
in Part II. Act II. Sc. iv:

> Now walk the angels on the walls of heaven,
> As sentinels to warn th' immortal souls
> To entertain divine Zenocrate.

This is not Spenser's movement, but the influence
of Spenser must be present. There had been no
great blank verse before Marlowe; but there was
the powerful presence of this great master of melody
immediately precedent; and the combination produced results which could not be repeated. I do not
think that it can be claimed that Peele had any influence here.

The passage quoted from Spenser has a further
interest. It will be noted that the fourth line:

> With blooms more white than Erycina's brows,

is Marlowe's contribution. Compare this with these
other lines of Marlowe:

> So looks my love, shadowing in her brows
> (Tamburlaine)
> Like to the shadows of Pyramides
> (Tamburlaine)

and the final and best version:

> Shadowing more beauty in their airy brows
> Than have the white breasts of the queen of love
> (Doctor Faustus)

and compare the whole set with Spenser again
(*F.Q.*):

> *Upon her eyelids many graces sate*
> *Under the shadow of her even brows,*

a passage which Mr. Robertson says Spenser himself
used in three other places.

This economy is frequent in Marlowe. Within
Tamburlaine it occurs in the form of monotony,
especially in the facile use of resonant names (e.g.
the recurrence of 'Caspia' or 'Caspian' with the
same tone effect), a practice in which Marlowe was
followed by Milton, but which Marlowe himself
outgrew. Again,

> *Zenocrate, lovelier than the love of Jove,*
> *Brighter than is the silver Rhodope,*

is paralleled later by

> *Zenocrate, the lovliest maid alive,*
> *Fairer than rocks of pearl and precious stone.*

One line Marlowe remodels with triumphant success:

> *And set black streamers in the firmament*
> > *(Tamburlaine)*

becomes

> *See, see, where Christ's blood streams in the firmament!*
> > *(Doctor Faustus)*

The verse accomplishments of *Tamburlaine* are notably two: Marlowe gets into blank verse the melody of Spenser, and he gets a new driving power by reinforcing the sentence period against the line period. The rapid long sentence, running line into line, as in the famous soliloquies 'Nature compounded of four elements' and 'What is beauty, saith my sufferings, then?' marks the certain escape of blank verse from the rhymed couplet, and from the elegiac or rather pastoral note of Surrey, to which Tennyson returned. If you contrast these two soliloquies with the verse of Marlowe's greatest contemporary, Kyd—by no means a despicable versifier —you see the importance of the innovation:

> *The one took sanctuary, and, being sent for out,*
> *Was murdered in Southwark as he passed*
> *To Greenwich, where the Lord Protector lay.*
> *Black Will was burned in Flushing on a stage;*
> *Green was hanged at Osbridge in Kent . . .*

which is not really inferior to:

> *So these four abode*
> *Within one house together; and as years*
> *Went forward, Mary took another mate;*
> *But Dora lived unmarried till her death.*
> (TENNYSON, *Dora*)

In *Faustus* Marlowe went further: he broke up the

line, to a gain in intensity, in the last soliloquy; and he developed a new and important conversational tone in the dialogues of *Faustus* with the devil. *Edward II* has never lacked consideration: it is more desirable, in brief space, to remark upon two plays, one of which has been misunderstood and the other underrated. These are the *Jew of Malta* and *Dido Queen of Carthage*. Of the first of these, it has always been said that the end, even the last two acts, are unworthy of the first three. If one takes the *Jew of Malta* not as a tragedy, or as a 'tragedy of blood', but as a farce, the concluding act becomes intelligible; and if we attend with a careful ear to the versification, we find that Marlowe develops a tone to suit this farce, and even perhaps that this tone is his most powerful and mature tone. I say farce, but with the enfeebled humour of our times the word is a misnomer; it is the farce of the old English humour, the terribly serious, even savage comic humour, the humour which spent its last breath in the decadent genius of Dickens. It has nothing in common with J. M. Barrie, Captain Bairnsfather, or *Punch*. It is the humour of that very serious (but very different) play, *Volpone*.

> *First, be thou void of these affections,*
> *Compassion, love, vain hope, and heartless fear;*
> *Be moved at nothing, see thou pity none . . .*

As for myself, I walk abroad o' nights,
And kill sick people groaning under walls,
Sometimes I go about and poison wells . . .

and the last words of Barabas complete this prodigious caricature:

But now begins th' extremity of heat
To pinch me with intolerable pangs
Die, life! fly, soul! tongue, curse thy fill, and die!

It is something which Shakespeare could not do,
and which he did not want to do.

Dido appears to be a hurried play, perhaps done
to order with the *Æneid* in front of him. But even
here there is progress. The account of the sack of
Troy is in this newer style of Marlowe's, this style
which secures its emphasis by always hesitating on
the edge of caricature at the right moment:

The Grecian soldiers, tir'd with ten years war,
Began to cry, 'Let us unto our ships,
Troy is invincible, why stay we here?' . . .

By this, the camp was come unto the walls,
And through the breach did march into the streets,
Where, meeting with the rest, 'Kill, kill!' they
    cried. . . .

And after him, his band of Myrmidons,
With balls of wild-fire in their murdering paws . . .

At last, the soldiers pull'd her by the heels,
And swung her howling in the empty air. . . .

We saw Cassandra sprawling in the streets . . .

This is not Virgil, or Shakespeare; it is pure Marlowe. By comparing the whole speech with Clarence's dream, in *Richard III*, one acquires a little insight into the difference between Marlowe and Shakespeare:

> *What scourge for perjury*
> *Can this dark monarchy afford false Clarence?*

There, on the other hand, is what Marlowe's style could not do; the phrase has a concision which is almost classical, certainly Dantesque. Again, as often with the Elizabethan dramatists, there are lines in Marlowe, besides the many lines that Shakespeare adapted, that might have been written by either:

> *If thou wilt stay,*
> *Leap in mine arms; mine arms are open wide;*
> *If not, turn from me, and I'll turn from thee;*
> *For though thou hast the heart to say farewell,*
> *I have not power to stay thee.*

But the direction in which Marlowe's verse might have moved, had he not 'dyed swearing', is quite un-Shakespearian, is toward this intense and serious and indubitably great poetry, which, like some great painting and sculpture, attains its effects by something not unlike caricature.

SHAKESPEARE AND THE
STOICISM OF SENECA

The last few years have witnessed a number of recrudescences of Shakespeare. There is the fatigued Shakespeare, a retired Anglo-Indian, presented by Mr. Lytton Strachey; there is the messianic Shakespeare, bringing a new philosophy and a new system of yoga, presented by Mr. Middleton Murry; and there is the ferocious Shakespeare, a furious Samson, presented by Mr. Wyndham Lewis in his interesting book, *The Lion and the Fox*. On the whole we may all agree that these manifestations are beneficial. In any case, so important as that of Shakespeare, it is good that we should from time to time change our minds. The last conventional Shakespeare is banished from the scene, and a variety of unconventional Shakespeares takes his place. About anyone so great as Shakespeare, it is probable that we can never be right; and if we can never be right, it is better that we should from time to time change our way of being wrong. Whether Truth ultimately prevails is doubtful and has never been proved; but it is certain that nothing is more effective in driving out error than a new error. Whether Mr. Strachey, or Mr. Murry, or Mr. Lewis, is any nearer to the truth of Shakespeare than Rymer, or Morgann, or Webster, or Johnson, is uncertain; they are all certainly more sympathetic in this year 1927 than Coleridge, or Swinburne, or Dowden. If they do not give us the real Shakespeare—if there is one—they at least give us several up-to-date Shakespeares. If the only way to prove that Shakespeare did not feel and think exactly as people felt and thought in 1815, or in 1860, or in 1880, is to show that he felt and thought as we felt and thought in 1927, then we must accept gratefully that alternative.

But these recent interpreters of Shakespeare suggest a number of reflections on literary criticism and its limits, on general æsthetics, and on the limitations of the human understanding.

There are, of course, a number of other current interpretations of Shakespeare: that is, of the *conscious opinions* of Shakespeare: interpretations of category, so to speak: which make him either a Tory journalist or a Liberal journalist, or a Socialist journalist (though Mr. Shaw has done something to warn off his co-religionists from claiming Shakespeare, or from finding anything uplifting in his work); we have also a Protestant Shakespeare, and a sceptical Shakespeare, and some case may be made out for an Anglo-Catholic, or even a Papist Shakespeare. My own frivolous opinion is that Shakespeare may have held in private life very different views from what we extract from his extremely varied published works; that there is no clue in his writings to the way in which he would have voted in the last or would vote in the next election; and that we are completely in the dark as to his attitude about prayer-book revision. I admit that my own experience, as a minor poet, may have jaundiced my outlook; that I am used to having cosmic significances, which I never suspected, extracted from my work (such as it is) by enthusiastic persons at a distance; and to being informed that something which I meant seriously is *vers de société*; and to having my personal biography reconstructed from passages which I got out of books, or which I invented out of nothing because they sounded well; and to having my biography invariably ignored in what I *did* write from personal experience; so that in consequence I am inclined to believe that people are mistaken about Shakespeare just in proportion to the relative superiority of Shakespeare to myself.

One more personal 'note': I believe that I have as high an estimate of the greatness of Shakespeare as poet and dramatist as anyone living; I certainly believe that there is nothing greater. And I would say that my only qualification for venturing to talk about him is, that I am *not* under the delusion that Shakespeare in the least resembles myself, either as I am or as I should like to imagine myself. It seems to me that one of the chief reasons for questioning Mr. Strachey's Shakespeare, and Mr. Murry's, and Mr. Lewis's, is the remarkable resemblance which they bear to Mr. Strachey, and Mr. Murry, and Mr. Lewis respectively. I have not a very clear idea of what Shakespeare was like. But I do not conceive him as very like either Mr. Strachey, or Mr. Murry, or Mr. Wyndham Lewis, or myself.

We have had Shakespeare explained by a variety of influences. He is explained by Montaigne, and by Machiavelli. I imagine that Mr. Strachey would explain Shakespeare by Montaigne, though this would also be Mr. Strachey's Montaigne (for all of Mr. Strachey's favourite figures have a strong Strachey physiognomy) and not Mr. Robertson's. I think that Mr. Lewis, in the intensely interesting book mentioned, has done a real service in calling attention to the importance of Machiavelli in Elizabethan England, though this Machiavelli be only the Machiavelli of the *Contre-Machiavel*, and not in the least the real Machiavelli, a person whom Elizabethan England was as incapable of understanding as Georgian England, or any England, is. I think, however, that Mr. Lewis has gone quite wrong if he

thinks (I am not sure what he thinks) that Shakespeare, and Elizabethan England in general, was
'influenced' by the thought of Machiavelli. I think
that Shakespeare, and other dramatists, used the
popular Machiavellian idea, for stage purposes; but
this idea was no more like Machiavelli, who was an
Italian and a Roman Christian, than Mr. Shaw's
idea of Nietzsche—whatever that is—is like the real
Nietzsche.

I propose a Shakespeare under the influence of the
stoicism of Seneca. But I do not believe that Shakespeare was under the influence of Seneca. I propose
it largely because I believe that after the Montaigne
Shakespeare (not that Montaigne had any philosophy whatever) and after the Machiavelli Shakespeare, a stoical or Senecan Shakespeare is almost
certain to be produced. I wish merely to disinfect
the Senecan Shakespeare before he appears. My ambitions would be realized if I could prevent him, in
so doing, from appearing at all.

I want to be quite definite in my notion of the
possible influence of Seneca on Shakespeare. I think
it is quite likely that Shakespeare read some of
Seneca's tragedies at school. I think it quite unlikely
that Shakespeare knew anything of that extraordin-
arily dull and uninteresting body of Seneca's prose,
which was translated by Lodge and printed in 1612.
So far as Shakespeare was influenced by Seneca, it

was by his memories of school conning and through the influence of the Senecan tragedy of the day, through Kyd and Peele, but chiefly Kyd. That Shakespeare deliberately took a 'view of life' from Seneca there seems to be no evidence whatever.

Nevertheless, there is, in some of the great tragedies of Shakespeare, a new attitude. It is not the attitude of Seneca, but is derived from Seneca; it is slightly different from anything that can be found in French tragedy, in Corneille or in Racine; it is modern, and it culminates, if there is ever any culmination, in the attitude of Nietzsche. I cannot say that it is Shakespeare's 'philosophy'. Yet many people have lived by it; though it may only have been Shakespeare's instinctive recognition of something of theatrical utility. It is the attitude of self-dramatization assumed by some of Shakespeare's heroes at moments of tragic intensity. It is not peculiar to Shakespeare; it is conspicuous in Chapman: Bussy, Clermont and Biron, all die in this way. Marston—one of the most interesting and least explored of all the Elizabethans—uses it; and Marston and Chapman were particularly Senecan. But Shakespeare, of course, does it very much better than any of the others, and makes it somehow more integral with the human nature of his characters. It is less verbal, more real. I have always felt that I have never read a more terrible exposure of human weakness—of universal human weakness—than the last great speech of Othello. (I am ignorant whether anyone else has ever adopted this view, and it may appear subjective and fantastic in the extreme.) It is usually taken on its face value, as expressing the greatness in defeat of a noble but erring nature.

> *Soft you; a word or two before you go.*
> *I have done the state some service, and they know't.*
> *No more of that. I pray you, in your letters,*
> *When you shall these unlucky deeds relate,*
> *Speak of me as I am; nothing extenuate,*
> *Nor set down aught in malice: then you must speak*
> *Of one that loved not wisely but too well;*
> *Of one not easily jealous, but, being wrought,*
> *Perplex'd in the extreme; of one whose hand,*
> *Like the base Indian, threw a pearl away*
> *Richer than all his tribe; of one whose subdued eyes,*
> *Albeit unused to the melting mood,*
> *Drop tears as fast as the Arabian trees*
> *Their medicinal gum. Set you down this;*
> *And say, besides, that in Aleppo once,*
> *Where a malignant and a turban'd Turk*
> *Beat a Venetian and traduced the state,*
> *I took by the throat the circumcized dog,*
> *And smote him, thus.*

What Othello seems to me to be doing in making this speech is *cheering himself up*. He is endeavouring to escape reality, he has ceased to think about Desdemona, and is thinking about himself. Humility is the most difficult of all virtues to achieve; nothing dies harder than the desire to think well of oneself. Othello succeeds in turning himself into a pathetic figure, by adopting an *æsthetic* rather than a moral attitude, dramatizing himself against his environment. He takes in the spectator, but the human motive is primarily to take in himself. I do not believe that any writer has ever exposed this *bovarysme*, the human will to see things as they are not, more clearly than Shakespeare.

If you compare the deaths of several of Shakespeare's heroes—I do not say *all*, for there are very few generalizations that can be applied to the whole of Shakespeare's work—but notably Othello, Coriolanus and Antony—with the deaths of heroes of dramatists such as Marston and Chapman, consciously under Senecan influence, you will find a strong similarity—except only that Shakespeare does it both more poetically and more lifelike.

You may say that Shakespeare is merely illustrating, consciously or unconsciously, human nature, not Seneca. But I am not so much concerned with the influence of Seneca on Shakespeare as with Shakespeare's illustration of Senecan and stoical principles. Much of Chapman's Senecanism has lately been shown by Professor Schoell to be directly borrowed from Erasmus and other sources. I am concerned with the fact that Seneca is the *literary* representative of Roman stoicism, and that Roman stoicism is an important ingredient in Elizabethan drama. It was natural that in a time like that of Elizabeth stoicism should appear. The original stoicism, and especially the Roman stoicism, was of course a philosophy suited to slaves: hence its absorption into early Christianity.

> *A man to join himself with the Universe*
> *In his main sway, and make in all things fit——*

A man does not join himself with the Universe so long as he has anything else to join himself with; men who could take part in the life of a thriving Greek city-state had something better to join themselves to; and Christians have had something better. Stoicism is the refuge for the individual in an indifferent or hostile world too big for him; it is the permanent substratum of a number of versions of cheering oneself up. Nietzsche is the most conspicuous modern instance of cheering oneself up. The stoical attitude is the reverse of Christian humility.

In Elizabethan England we have conditions apparently utterly different from those of imperial Rome. But it was a period of dissolution and chaos; and in such a period any emotional attitude which seems to give a man something firm, even if it be only the attitude of 'I am myself alone', is eagerly taken up. I hardly need—and it is beyond my present scope— to point out how readily, in a period like the Elizabethan, the Senecan attitude of Pride, the Montaigne attitude of Scepticism, and the Machiavelli attitude[1] of Cynicism, arrived at a kind of fusion in the Elizabethan individualism.

This individualism, this vice of Pride, was, of course, exploited largely because of its dramatic possibilities. But other drama had before existed without depending on this human failing. You do not find it in *Polyeucte*, or in *Phèdre* either. But even Hamlet, who has made a pretty considerable mess of things, and occasioned the death of at least three innocent people, and two more insignificant ones, dies fairly well pleased with himself——

> *Horatio, I am dead;*
> *Thou liv'st; report me and my cause aright*
> *To the unsatisfied. . . .*
> *O good Horatio, what a wounded name,*
> *Things standing thus unknown, shall live behind*
> *me!*

Antony says, 'I am Antony still', and the Duchess, 'I

---

[1] I do not mean the attitude of Machiavelli, which is not cynical. I mean the attitude of Englishmen who had heard of Machiavelli.

am Duchess of Malfy still'; would either of them have said that unless Medea had said *Medea superest*?

I do not wish to appear to maintain that the Elizabethan hero and the Senecan hero are identical. The influence of Seneca is much more apparent in the Elizabethan drama than it is in the plays of Seneca. The influence of any man is a different thing from himself. The Elizabethan hero is much more stoical and Senecan, in this way, than the Senecan hero. For Seneca was following the Greek tradition, which was not stoical; he developed familiar themes and imitated great models; so that the vast difference between his emotional attitude and that of the Greeks is rather latent in his work, and more apparent in the work of the Renaissance. And the Elizabethan hero, the hero of Shakespeare, was not invariable even in Elizabethan England. A notable exception is Faustus. Marlowe—not excepting Shakespeare or Chapman, the most *thoughtful* and philosophic mind, though immature, among the Elizabethan dramatists—could conceive the proud hero, as Tamburláine, but also the hero who has reached that point of horror at which even pride is abandoned. In a recent book on Marlowe, Miss Ellis-Fermor has put very well this peculiarity of Faustus, from another point of view than mine, but in words from which I take support:

'Marlowe follows Faustus further across the bor-

derline between consciousness and dissolution than
do any of his contemporaries. With Shakespeare,
with Webster, death is a sudden severing of life;
their men die, conscious to the last of some part at
least of their surroundings, influenced, even upheld,
by that consciousness and preserving the personality
and characteristics they have possessed through life.
. . . In Marlowe's Faustus alone all this is set aside.
He penetrates deeply into the experience of a mind
isolated from the past, absorbed in the realization of
its own destruction.'

But Marlowe, the most thoughtful, the most blas-
phemous (and therefore, probably, the most
Christian) of his contemporaries, is always an exception. Shakespeare is exceptional primarily by his
immense superiority.

Of all of Shakespeare's plays, *King Lear* is often
taken as the most Senecan in spirit. Cunliffe finds it
to be imbued with a Senecan fatalism. Here, again,
we must distinguish between a man and his influence. The differences between the fatalism of Greek
tragedy, and the fatalism of Seneca's tragedies, and
the fatalism of the Elizabethans, proceed by delicate
shades; there is a continuity, and there is also a violent contrast, when we look at them from far off. In
Seneca, the Greek ethics is visible underneath the
Roman stoicism. In the Elizabethans, the Roman
stoicism is visible beneath the Renaissance anarch-

ism. In *King Lear* there are several significant phrases, such as those which caught the attention of Professor Cunliffe, and there is a tone of Senecan fatalism: *fatis agimur*. But there is much less and much more. And this is the point at which I must part company with Mr. Wyndham Lewis. Mr. Lewis proposes a Shakespeare who is a *positive* nihilist, an intellectual force *willing* destruction. I cannot see in Shakespeare either a deliberate scepticism, as of Montaigne, or a deliberate cynicism, as of Machiavelli, or a deliberate resignation, as of Seneca. I can see that he *used* all of these things, for dramatic ends: you get perhaps more Montaigne in *Hamlet,* and more Machiavelli in *Othello,* and more Seneca in *Lear.* But I cannot agree with the following paragraph:

'With the exception of Chapman, Shakespeare is the only thinker we meet with among the Elizabethan dramatists. By this is meant, of course that his work contained, apart from poetry, phantasy, rhetoric or observation of manners, a body of matter representing explicit processes of the intellect which would have furnished a moral philosopher like Montaigne with the natural material for his essays. But the quality of this thinking—as it can be surprised springing naturally in the midst of the consummate movements of his art—is, as must be the case with such a man, of startling force some-

times. And if it is not systematic, at least a recogniz-
able physiognomy is there.'

It is this general notion of 'thinking' that I would
challenge. One has the difficulty of having to use the
same words for different things. We say, in a vague
way, that Shakespeare, or Dante, or Lucretius, is a
poet who thinks, and that Swinburne is a poet who
does not think, even that Tennyson is a poet who
does not think. But what we really mean is not a
difference in quality of thought, but a difference in
quality of emotion. The poet who 'thinks' is merely
the poet who can express the emotional equivalent
of thought. But he is not necessarily interested in the
thought itself. We talk as if thought was precise and
emotion was vague. In reality there is precise emotion and there is vague emotion. To express precise
emotion requires as great intellectual power as to
express precise thought. But by 'thinking' I mean
something very different from anything that I find
in Shakespeare. Mr. Lewis, and other champions of
Shakespeare as a great philosopher, have a great deal
to say about Shakespeare's power of thought, but
they fail to show that he thought to any purpose;
that he had any coherent view of life, or that he
recommended any procedure to follow. 'We possess a great deal of evidence', says Mr. Lewis, 'as to
what Shakespeare thought of military glory and
martial events.' Do we? Or rather, did Shakespeare

think anything at all? He was occupied with turning human actions into poetry.

I would suggest that none of the plays of Shakespeare has a 'meaning', although it would be equally false to say that a play of Shakespeare is meaningless. All great poetry gives the illusion of a view of life. When we enter into the world of Homer, or Sophocles, or Virgil, or Dante, or Shakespeare, we incline to believe that we are apprehending something that can be expressed intellectually; for every precise emotion tends towards intellectual formulation.

We are apt to be deluded by the example of Dante. Here, we think, is a poem which represents an exact intellectual system; Dante has a 'philosophy', therefore every poet as great as Dante has a philosophy too. Dante had behind him the system of St. Thomas, to which his poem corresponds point to point. Therefore Shakespeare had behind him Seneca, or Montaigne, or Machiavelli; and if his work does not correspond point to point with any or a composition of these, then it must be that he did a little quiet thinking on his own, and was better than any of these people at their own job. I can see no reason for believing that either Dante or Shakespeare did any thinking on his own. The people who think that Shakespeare thought, are always people who are not engaged in writing poetry, but who are engaged in thinking, and we all like to think that

great men were like ourselves. The difference between Shakespeare and Dante is that Dante had one
coherent system of thought behind him; but that
was just his luck, and from the point of view of
poetry is an irrelevant accident. It happened that at
Dante's time thought was orderly and strong and
beautiful, and that it was concentrated in one man
of the greatest genius; Dante's poetry receives a
boost which in a sense it does not merit, from the
fact that the thought behind it is the thought of a
man as great and lovely as Dante himself: St.
Thomas. The thought behind Shakespeare is of men
far inferior to Shakespeare himself: hence the alternative errors, first, that as Shakespeare was as great
a poet as Dante, he must have supplied, out of his
own thinking, the difference in quality between a
St. Thomas and a Montaigne or a Machiavelli or a
Seneca, or second, that Shakespeare is inferior to
Dante. In truth neither Shakespeare nor Dante did
any real thinking—that was not their job; and the
relative value of the thought current at their time,
the material enforced upon each to use as the vehicle
of his feeling, is of no importance. It does not make
Dante a greater poet, or mean that we can learn
more from Dante than from Shakespeare. We can
certainly learn more from Aquinas than from
Seneca, but that is quite a different matter. When
Dante says *la sua voluntade e nostra pace*

it is great poetry, and there is a great philosophy behind it. When Shakespeare says

As flies to wanton boys, are we to the gods;
They kill us for their sport,

it is *equally* great poetry, though the philosophy behind it is not great. But the essential is that each expresses in perfect language, some permanent human impulse. Emotionally, the latter is just as strong, just as true, and just as informative—just as useful and beneficial in the sense in which poetry is useful and beneficial, as the former.

What every poet starts from is his own emotions. And when we get down to these, there is not much to choose between Shakespeare and Dante. Dante's railings, his personal spleen—sometimes thinly disguised under Old Testamental prophetic denunciations—his nostalgia, his bitter regrets for past happiness—or for what seems happiness when it is past—and his brave attempts to fabricate something permanent and holy out of his personal animal feelings —as in the *Vita Nuova*—can all be matched out of Shakespeare. Shakespeare, too, was occupied with the struggle—which alone constitutes life for a poet —to transmute his personal and private agonies into something rich and strange, something universal and impersonal. The rage of Dante against Florence, or Pistoia, or what not, the deep surge of Shakespeare's general cynicism and disillusionment, are merely gigantic attempts to metamorphose private failures and disappointments. The great poet, in writing himself, writes his time.[1] Thus Dante, hardly knowing it, became the voice of the thirteenth century; Shakespeare, hardly knowing it, became the representative of the end of the sixteenth century, of a turning point in history. But you can hardly say that Dante believed, or did not believe, the Thomist philosophy; you can hardly say that Shakespeare believed, or did not believe, the mixed and muddled scepticism of the Renaissance. If Shakespeare had written according to a better philosophy, he would have written worse poetry; it was his business to express the greatest emotional intensity of his time, based on whatever his time happened to think. Poetry is not a substitute for philosophy or theology or religion, as Mr. Lewis and Mr. Murry sometimes seem to think; it has its own function. But as this function is not intellectual but emotional, it cannot be defined adequately in intellectual terms. We can say that it provides 'consolation': strange consolation, which is provided equally by writers so different as Dante and Shakespeare.

What I have said could be expressed more exactly,

[1] Remy de Gourmont said much the same thing, in speaking of Flaubert.

but at much greater length, in philosophical language: it would enter into the department of philosophy which might be called the Theory of Belief (which is not psychology but philosophy, or phenomenology proper)—the department in which Meinong and Husserl have made some pioneer investigation; the different meanings which belief has in different minds according to the activity for which they are oriented. I doubt whether belief proper enters into the activity of a great poet, *qua* poet. That is, Dante, *qua* poet, did not believe or disbelieve the Thomist cosmology or theory of the soul: he merely made use of it, or a fusion took place between his initial emotional impulses and a theory, for the purpose of making poetry. The poet makes poetry, the metaphysician makes metaphysics, the bee makes honey, the spider secretes a filament; you can hardly say that any of these agents believes: he merely does.

The problem of belief is very complicated and probably quite insoluble. We must make allowance for differences in the emotional quality of believing not only between persons of different occupation, such as the philosopher and the poet, but between different periods of time. The end of the sixteenth century is an epoch when it is particularly difficult to associate poetry with systems of thought or reasoned views of life. In making some very commonplace investigations of the 'thought' of Donne, I found it quite impossible to come to the conclusion that Donne believed anything. It seemed as if, at that time, the world was filled with broken fragments of systems, and that a man like Donne merely picked up, like a magpie, various shining fragments of ideas as they struck his eye, and stuck them about here and there in his verse. Miss Ramsay, in her learned and exhaustive study of Donne's sources, came to the conclusion that he was a 'mediæval thinker'; I could not find either any 'mediævalism' or any thinking, but only a vast jumble of incoherent erudition on which he drew for purely poetic effects. The recent work of Professor Schoell on the sources of Chapman seems to show Chapman engaged in the same task; and suggests that the 'profundity' and 'obscurity' of Chapman's dark thinking are largely due to his lifting long passages from the works of writers like Ficino and incorporating them in his poems completely out of their context.

I do not for a moment suggest that the method of Shakespeare was anything like this. Shakespeare was a much finer instrument for transformations than any of his contemporaries, finer perhaps even than Dante. He also needed less contact in order to be able to absorb all that he required. The element of Seneca is the most completely absorbed and transmogrified, because it was already the most diffused throughout Shakespeare's world. The element of Machiavelli is probably the most indirect, the element of Montaigne the most immediate. It has been said that Shakespeare lacks unity; it might, I think, be said equally well that it is Shakespeare chiefly that *is* the unity, that unifies so far as they could be unified all the tendencies of a time that certainly lacked unity. Unity, in Shakespeare, but not universality; no one can be universal: Shakespeare would not have found much in common with his contemporary St. Theresa. What influence the work of Seneca and Machiavelli and Montaigne seems to me to exert in common on that time, and most conspicuously through Shakespeare, is an influence toward a kind of self-consciousness that is new; the self-consciousness and self-dramatization of the Shakespearian hero, of whom Hamlet is only one. It seems to mark a stage, even if not a very agreeable one, in human history, or progress, or deterioration, or change. Roman stoicism was in its own time a development in self-consciousness; taken up into Christianity, it broke loose again in the dissolution of the Renaissance. Nietzsche, as I suggested, is a late variant: his attitude is a kind of stoicism upside-down: for there is not much difference between identifying oneself with the Universe and identifying the Universe with oneself. The influence of Seneca on Elizabethan drama has been exhaustively studied in its formal aspect, and in the borrowing and adaptation of phrases and situations; the penetration of Senecan sensibility would be much more difficult to trace.

HAMLET

Few critics have ever admitted that *Hamlet* the play is the primary problem, and Hamlet the character only secondary. And Hamlet the character has had an especial temptation for that most dangerous type of critic: the critic with a mind which is naturally of the creative order, but which through some weakness in creative power exercises itself in criticism instead. These minds often find in Hamlet a vicarious existence for their own artistic realization. Such a mind had Goethe, who made of Hamlet a Werther; and such had Coleridge, who made of Hamlet a Coleridge; and probably neither of these men in writing about Hamlet remembered that his first business was to study a work of art. The kind of criticism that Goethe and Coleridge produced, in writing of Hamlet, is the most misleading kind possible. For they both possessed unquestionable critical insight, and both make their critical aberrations the more plausible by the substitution—

but he did

of their own Hamlet for Shakespeare's—which their creative gift effects. We should be thankful that Walter Pater did not fix his attention on this play.

Two writers of our time, Mr. J. M. Robertson and Professor Stoll of the University of Minnesota, have issued small books which can be praised for moving in the other direction. Mr. Stoll performs a service in recalling to our attention the labours of the critics of the seventeenth and eighteenth centuries,[1] observing that

'they knew less about psychology than more recent Hamlet critics, but they were nearer in spirit to Shakespeare's art; and as they insisted on the importance of the effect of the whole rather than on the importance of the leading character, they were nearer, in their old-fashioned way, to the secret of dramatic art in general.'

Qua work of art, the work of art cannot be interpreted; there is nothing to interpret; we can only criticize it according to standards, in comparison to other works of art; and for 'interpretation' the chief task is the presentation of relevant historical fact which the reader is not assumed to know. Mr. Robertson points out, very pertinently, how critics have failed in their 'interpretation' of *Hamlet* by ignoring what ought to be very obvious: that *Hamlet*

---

[1] I have never, by the way, seen a cogent refutation of Thomas Rymer's objections to *Othello*.

is a stratification, that it represents the efforts of a series of men, each making what he could out of the work of his predecessors. The *Hamlet* of Shakespeare will appear to us very differently if, instead of treating the whole action of the play as due to Shakespeare's design, we perceive his *Hamlet* to be superposed upon much cruder material which persists even in the final form.

We know that there was an older play by Thomas Kyd, that extraordinary dramatic (if not poetic) genius who was in all probability the author of two plays so dissimilar as the *Spanish Tragedy* and *Arden of Feversham*; and what this play was like we can guess from three clues: from the *Spanish Tragedy* itself, from the tale of Belleforest upon which Kyd's *Hamlet* must have been based, and from a version acted in Germany in Shakespeare's lifetime which bears strong evidence of having been adapted from the earlier, not from the later, play. From these three sources it is clear that in the earlier play the motive was a revenge motive simply; that the action or delay is caused, as in the *Spanish Tragedy*, solely by the difficulty of assassinating a monarch surrounded by guards; and that the 'madness' of Hamlet was feigned in order to escape suspicion, and successfully. In the final play of Shakespeare, on the other hand, there is a motive which is more important than that of revenge, and which explicitly 'blunts' the latter; the delay in revenge is unexplained on grounds of necessity or expediency; and the effect of the 'madness' is not to lull but to arouse the king's suspicion. The alteration is not complete enough, however, to be convincing. Furthermore, there are verbal parallels so close to the *Spanish Tragedy* as to leave no doubt that in places Shakespeare was merely *revising* the text of Kyd. And finally there are unexplained scenes—the Polonius-Laertes and the Polonius-Reynaldo scenes—for which there is little excuse; these scenes are not in the verse style of Kyd, and not beyond doubt in the style of Shakespeare. These Mr. Robertson believes to be scenes in the original play of Kyd reworked by a third hand, perhaps Chapman, before Shakespeare touched the play. And he concludes, with very strong show of reason, that the original play of Kyd was, like certain other revenge plays, in two parts of five acts each. The upshot of Mr. Robertson's examination is, we believe, irrefragible: that Shakespeare's *Hamlet*, so far as it is Shakespeare's, is a play dealing with the effect of a mother's guilt upon her son, and that Shakespeare was unable to impose this motive successfully upon the 'intractable' material of the old play.

Of the intractability there can be no doubt. So far from being Shakespeare's masterpiece, the play is most certainly an artistic failure. In several ways the play is puzzling, and disquieting as is none of the others. Of all the plays it is the longest and is possibly the one on which Shakespeare spent most pains; and yet he has left in it superfluous and inconsistent scenes which even hasty revision should have noticed. The versification is variable. Lines like

> *Look, the morn, in russet mantle clad,*
> *Walks o'er the dew of yon high eastern hill,*

are of the Shakespeare of *Romeo and Juliet*. The lines in Act V. Sc. ii,

> *Sir, in my heart there was a kind of fighting*
> *That would not let me sleep . . .*
> *Up from my cabin,*
> *My sea-gown scarf'd about me, in the dark*
> *Grop'd I to find out them, had my desire;*
> *Finger'd their packet;*

are of his quite mature. Both workmanship and thought are in an unstable position. We are surely justified in attributing the play, with that other profoundly interesting play of 'intractable' material and astonishing versification, *Measure for Measure*, to a period of crisis, after which follow the tragic successes which culminate in *Coriolanus*. *Coriolanus* may be not as 'interesting' as *Hamlet*, but it is, with *Antony and Cleopatra*, Shakespeare's most assured artistic success. And probably more people have thought *Hamlet* a work of art because they found it interesting, than have found it interesting because it is a work of art. It is the 'Mona Lisa' of literature.

The grounds of *Hamlet's* failure are not immediately obvious. Mr. Robertson is undoubtedly correct in concluding that the essential emotion of the play is the feeling of a son towards a guilty mother:

'[Hamlet's] tone is that of one who has suffered tortures on the score of his mother's degradation. . . . The guilt of a mother is an almost intolerable motive for drama, but it had to be maintained and emphasized to supply a psychological solution, or rather a hint of one.'

This, however, is by no means the whole story. It is not merely the 'guilt of a mother' that cannot be handled as Shakespeare handled the suspicion of Othello, the infatuation of Antony, or the pride of Coriolanus. The subject might conceivably have expanded into a tragedy like these, intelligible, self-complete, in the sunlight. *Hamlet*, like the sonnets, is full of some stuff that the writer could not drag to light, contemplate, or manipulate into art. And when we search for this feeling, we find it, as in the sonnets, very difficult to localize. You cannot point to it in the speeches; indeed, if you examine the two famous soliloquies you see the versification of Shakespeare, but a content which might be claimed by another, perhaps by the author of the *Revenge of*

Bussy d'Ambois, Act V. Sc. i. We find Shakespeare's *Hamlet* not in the action, not in any quotations that we might select, so much as in an un-
mistakable tone which is unmistakably not in the
earlier play.

The only way of expressing emotion in the form
of art is by finding an 'objective correlative'; in
other words, a set of objects, a situation, a chain of
events which shall be the formula of that *particular*
emotion; such that when the external facts, which
must terminate in sensory experience, are given, the
emotion is immediately evoked. If you examine any
of Shakespeare's more successful tragedies, you will
find this exact equivalence; you will find that the
state of mind of Lady Macbeth walking in her sleep
has been communicated to you by a skilful accumu-
lation of imagined sensory impressions; the words
of Macbeth on hearing of his wife's death strike us
as if, given the sequence of events, these words were
automatically released by the last event in the series.
The artistic 'inevitability' lies in this complete
adequacy of the external to the emotion; and this is
precisely what is deficient in *Hamlet*. Hamlet (the
man) is dominated by an emotion which is inexpres-
sible, because it is in *excess* of the facts as they appear.
And the supposed identity of Hamlet with his
author is genuine to this point: that Hamlet's bafflement at the absence of objective equivalent to his

feelings is a prolongation of the bafflement of his creator in the face of his artistic problem. Hamlet is up against the difficulty that his disgust is occasioned by his mother, but that his mother is not an adequate equivalent for it; his disgust envelops and exceeds her. It is thus a feeling which he cannot understand; he cannot objectify it, and it therefore remains to poison life and obstruct action. None of the possible actions can satisfy it; and nothing that Shakespeare can do with the plot can express Hamlet for him. And it must be noticed that the very nature of the *données* of the problem precludes objective equivalence. To have heightened the criminality of Gertrude would have been to provide the formula for a totally different emotion in Hamlet; it is just *because* her character is so negative and insignificant that she arouses in Hamlet the feeling which she is incapable of representing.

The 'madness' of Hamlet lay to Shakespeare's hand; in the earlier play a simple ruse, and to the end, we may presume, understood as a ruse by the audience. For Shakespeare it is less than madness and more than feigned. The levity of Hamlet, his repetition of phrase, his puns, are not part of a deliberate plan of dissimulation, but a form of emotional relief. In the character Hamlet it is the buffoonery of an emotion which can find no outlet in action; in the dramatist it is the buffoonery of an emotion which he cannot express in art. The intense feeling, ecstatic or terrible, without an object or exceeding its object, is something which every person of sensibility has known; it is doubtless a subject of study for pathologists. It often occurs in adolescence: the ordinary person puts these feelings to sleep, or trims down his feelings to fit the business world; the artist keeps them alive by his ability to intensify the world to his emotions. The Hamlet of Laforgue is an adolescent; the Hamlet of Shakespeare is not, he has not that explanation and excuse. We must simply admit that here Shakespeare tackled a problem which proved too much for him. Why he attempted it at all is an insoluble puzzle; under compulsion of what experience he attempted to express the inexpressibly horrible, we cannot ever know. We need a great many facts in his biography; and we should like to know whether, and when, and after or at the same time as what personal experience, he read Montaigne, II. xii, *Apologie de Raimond Sebond*. We should have, finally, to know something which is by hypothesis unknowable, for we assume it to be an experience which, in the manner indicated, exceeded the facts. We should have to understand things which Shakespeare did not understand himself.

BEN JONSON

The reputation of Jonson has been of the most deadly kind that can be compelled upon the memory of a great poet. To be universally accepted; to be damned by the praise that quenches all desire to read the book; to be afflicted by the imputation of the virtues which excite the least pleasure; and to be read only by historians and antiquaries—this is the most perfect conspiracy of approval. For some generations the reputation of Jonson has been carried rather as a liability than as an asset in the balance-sheet of English literature. No critic has succeeded in making him appear pleasurable or even interesting. Swinburne's book on Jonson satisfies no curiosity and stimulates no thought. For the critical study in the 'Men of Letters Series' by Mr. Gregory Smith there is a place; it satisfies curiosity, it supplies many just observations, it provides valuable matter on the neglected masques; it only fails to remodel the image of Jonson which is settled in our minds. Probably the fault lies with several generations of our poets. It is not that the value of poetry is only its value to living poets for their own work; but appreciation is akin to creation, and true enjoyment of poetry is related to the stirring of suggestion, the stimulus that a poet feels in his enjoyment of other poetry. Jonson has provided no creative stimulus for a very long time; consequently we must look back as far as Dryden—precisely, a poetic practitioner who learned from Jonson—before we find a living criticism of Jonson's work.

Yet there are possibilities for Jonson even now. We have no difficulty in seeing what brought him to this pass; how, in contrast, not with Shakespeare, but with Marlowe, Webster, Donne, Beaumont and Fletcher, he has been paid out with reputation instead of enjoyment. He is no less a poet than these men, but his poetry is of the surface. Poetry of the surface cannot be understood without study; for to deal with the surface of life, as Jonson dealt with it, is to deal so deliberately that we too must be deliberate, in order to understand. Shakespeare, and smaller men also, are in the end more difficult, but they offer something at the start to encourage the student or to satisfy those who want nothing more; they are suggestive, evocative, a phrase, a voice; they offer poetry in detail as well as in design. So does

Dante offer something, a phrase everywhere (*tu se'
ombra ed ombra vedi*) even to readers who have no
Italian; and Dante and Shakespeare have poetry of
design as well as of detail. But the polished veneer of
Jonson only reflects the lazy reader's fatuity; unconscious does not respond to unconscious; no
swarms of inarticulate feelings are aroused. The
immediate appeal of Jonson is to the mind; his emotional tone is not in the single verse, but in the design
of the whole. But not many people are capable of
discovering for themselves the beauty which is only
found after labour; and Jonson's industrious readers
have been those whose interest was historical and
curious, and those who have thought that in discovering the historical and curious interest they had
discovered the artistic value as well. When we say
that Jonson requires study, we do not mean study
of his classical scholarship or of seventeenth-century
manners. We mean intelligent saturation in his work
as a whole; we mean that, in order to enjoy him at
all, we must get to the centre of his work and his
temperament, and that we must see him unbiased by
time, as a contemporary. And to see him as a contemporary does not so much require the power of
putting ourselves into seventeenth-century London
as it requires the power of setting Jonson in our
London.

It is generally conceded that Jonson failed as a

tragic dramatist, and it is usually agreed that he failed because his genius was for satiric comedy and because of the weight of pedantic learning with which he burdened his two tragic failures. The second point marks an obvious error of detail; the first is too crude a statement to be accepted; to say that he failed because his genius was unsuited to tragedy is to tell us nothing at all. Jonson did not write a good tragedy, but we can see no reason why he should not have written one. If two plays so different as *The Tempest* and *The Silent Woman* are both comedies, surely the category of tragedy could be made wide enough to include something possible for Jonson to have done. But the classification of tragedy and comedy, while it may be sufficient to mark the distinction in a dramatic literature of more rigid form and treatment—it may distinguish Aristophanes from Euripides—is not adequate to a drama of such variations as the Elizabethans. Tragedy is a crude classification for plays so different in their tone as *Macbeth*, *The Jew of Malta*, and *The Witch of Edmonton*; and it does not help us much to say that *The Merchant of Venice* and *The Alchemist* are comedies. Jonson had his own scale, his own instrument. The merit which *Catiline* possesses is the same merit that is exhibited more triumphantly in *Volpone*; *Catiline* fails, not because it is too laboured and conscious, but because it is not conscious enough;

because Jonson in this play was not alert to his own idiom, not clear in his mind as to what his temperament wanted him to do. In *Catiline* Jonson conforms, or attempts to conform, to conventions; not to the conventions of antiquity, which he had exquisitely under control, but to the conventions of tragico-historical drama of his time. It is not the Latin erudition that sinks *Catiline*, but the application of that erudition to a form which was not the proper vehicle for the mind which had amassed the erudition.

If you look at *Catiline*—that dreary Pyrrhic victory of tragedy—you find two passages to be successful: Act II. Sc. i, the dialogue of the political ladies, and the Prologue of Sylla's ghost. These two passages are genial. The soliloquy of the ghost is a characteristic Jonson success in content and in versification—

> *Dost thou not feel me, Rome? not yet! is night*
> *So heavy on thee, and my weight so light?*
> *Can Sylla's ghost arise within thy walls,*
> *Less threatening than an earthquake, the quick falls*
> *Of thee and thine? Shake not the frighted heads*
> *Of thy steep towers, or shrink to their first beds?*
> *Or as their ruin the large Tyber fills,*
> *Make that swell up, and drown thy seven proud*
>   *hills? . . .*

This is the learned, but also the creative, Jonson. Without concerning himself with the character of Sulla, and in lines of invective, Jonson makes Sylla's ghost, while the words are spoken, a living and terrible force. The words fall with as determined beat as if they were the will of the morose Dictator himself. You may say: merely invective; but mere invective, even if as superior to the clumsy fisticuffs of Marston and Hall as Jonson's verse is superior to theirs, would not create a living figure as Jonson has done in this long tirade. And you may say: rhetoric; but if we are to call it 'rhetoric' we must subject that term to a closer dissection than any to which it is accustomed. What Jonson has done here is not merely a fine speech. It is the careful, precise filling in of a strong and simple outline, and at no point does it overflow the outline; it is far more careful and precise in its obedience to this outline than are many of the speeches in *Tamburlaine*. The outline is not Sulla, for Sulla has nothing to do with it, but 'Sylla's ghost'. The words may not be suitable to an historical Sulla, or to anybody in history, but they are a perfect expression for 'Sylla's ghost'. You cannot say they are rhetorical 'because people do not talk like that', you cannot call them 'verbiage'; they do not exhibit prolixity or redundancy or the other vices in the rhetoric books; there is a definite artistic emotion which demands expression at that length.

The words themselves are mostly simple words, the syntax is natural, the language austere rather than adorned. Turning then to the induction of *The Poetaster*, we find another success of the same kind:

Light, I salute thee, but with wounded nerves . . .

Men may not talk in that way, but the Spirit of Envy does, and in the words of Jonson Envy is a real and living person. It is not human life that informs Envy and Sylla's ghost, but it is energy of which human life is only another variety.

Returning to *Catiline*, we find that the best scene in the body of the play is one which cannot be squeezed into a tragic frame, and which appears to belong to satiric comedy. The scene between Fulvia and Galla and Sempronia is a living scene in a wilderness of oratory. And as it recalls other scenes—there is a suggestion of the college of ladies in *The Silent Woman*—it looks like a comedy scene. And it appears to be satire.

> *They shall all give and pay well, that come here,*
> *If they will have it; and that, jewels, pearl,*
> *Plate, or round sums to buy these. I'm not taken*
> *With a cob-swan or a high-mounting bull,*
> *As foolish Leda and Europa were;*
> *But the bright gold, with Danaë. For such price*
> *I would endure a rough, harsh Jupiter,*

Or ten such thundering gamesters, and refrain
To laugh at 'em, till they are gone, with my much
suffering.

This scene is no more comedy than it is tragedy, and
the 'satire' is merely a medium for the essential
emotion. Jonson's drama is only incidentally satire,
because it is only incidentally a criticism upon the
actual world. It is not satire in the way in which the
work of Swift or the work of Molière may be called
satire: that is, it does not find its source in any precise emotional attitude or precise intellectual criticism of the actual world. It is satire perhaps as the
work of Rabelais is satire; certainly not more so.
The important thing is that if fiction can be divided
into creative fiction and critical fiction, Jonson's is
creative. That he was a great critic, our first great
critic, does not affect this assertion. Every creator is
also a critic; Jonson was a conscious critic, but he
was also conscious in his creations. Certainly, one
sense in which the term 'critical' may be applied to
fiction is a sense in which the term might be used of
a method antithetical to Jonson's. It is the method
of *Education Sentimentale*. The characters of Jonson,
of Shakespeare, perhaps of all the greatest drama,
are drawn in positive and simple outlines. They may
be filled in, and by Shakespeare they are filled in, by
much detail or many shifting aspects; but a clear and

sharp and simple form remains through these—
though it would be hard to say in what the clarity
and sharpness and simplicity of Hamlet consists. But
Frédéric Moreau is not made in that way. He is constructed partly by negative definition, built up by a
great number of observations. We cannot isolate
him from the environment in which we find him;
it may be an environment which is or can be uni-
versalized; nevertheless it, and the figure in it, consist of very many observed particular facts, the
actual world. Without this world the figure dissolves.
The ruling faculty is a critical perception, a commentary upon experienced feeling and sensation. If
this is true of Flaubert, it is true in a higher degree of
Molière than of Jonson. The broad farcical lines of
Molière may seem to be the same drawing as Jonson's. But Molière—say in Alceste or Monsieur
Jourdain—is criticizing the actual; the reference to
the actual world is more direct. And having a more
tenuous reference, the work of Jonson is much less
directly satirical.

This leads us to the question of Humours. Largely
on the evidence of the two Humour plays, it is sometimes assumed that Jonson is occupied with types;
typical exaggerations, or exaggerations of type.
The Humour definition, the expressed intention of
Jonson, may be satisfactory for these two plays.
Every Man in his Humour is the first mature work of

Jonson, and the student of Jonson must study it; but it is not the play in which Jonson found his genius: it is the last of his plays to read first. If one reads *Volpone*, and after that re-reads the *Jew of Malta*; then returns to Jonson and reads *Bartholomew Fair*, *The Alchemist*, *Epicæne* and *The Devil is an Ass*, and finally *Catiline*, it is possible to arrive at a fair opinion of the poet and the dramatist.

The Humour, even at the beginning, is not a type, as in Marston's satire, but a simplified and somewhat distorted individual with a typical mania. In the later work, the Humour definition quite fails to account for the total effect produced. The characters of Shakespeare are such as might exist in different circumstances than those in which Shakespeare sets them. The latter appear to be those which extract from the characters the most intense and interesting realization; but that realization has not exhausted their possibilities. Volpone's life, on the other hand, is bounded by the scene in which it is played; in fact, the life is the life of the scene and is derivatively the life of Volpone; the life of the character is inseparable from the life of the drama. This is not dependence upon a background, or upon a substratum of fact. The emotional effect is single and simple. Whereas in Shakespeare the effect is due to the way in which the characters *act upon* one another, in Jonson it is given by the way in which the characters

74

fit in with each other. The artistic result of *Volpone* is not due to any effect that Volpone, Mosca, Corvino, Corbaccio, Voltore have upon each other, but simply to their combination into a whole. And these figures are not personifications of passions; separately, they have not even that reality, they are constituents. It is a similar indication of Jonson's method that you can hardly pick out a line of Jonson's and say confidently that it is great poetry; but there are many extended passages to which you cannot deny that honour.

> *I will have all my beds blown up, not stuft;*
> *Down is too hard; and then, mine oval room*
> *Fill'd with such pictures as Tiberius took*
> *From Elephantis, and dull Aretine*
> *But coldly imitated. Then, my glasses*
> *Cut in more subtle angles, to disperse*
> *And multiply the figures, as I walk. . . .*

Jonson is the legitimate heir of Marlowe. The man who wrote, in *Volpone*:

> *for thy love,*
> *In varying figures, I would have contended*
> *With the blue Proteus, or the hornèd flood. . . .*

and

> *See, a carbuncle*
> *May put out both the eyes of our Saint Mark;*

75

A diamond would have bought Lollia Paulina,
When she came in like star-light, hid with jewels. . . .

is related to Marlowe as a poet; and if Marlowe is a
poet, Jonson is also. And, if Jonson's comedy is a
comedy of humours, then Marlowe's tragedy, a
large part of it, is a tragedy of humours. But Jonson
has too exclusively been considered as the typical
representative of a point of view toward comedy.
He has suffered from his great reputation as a critic
and theorist, from the effects of his intelligence. We
have been taught to think of him as the man, the
dictator (confusedly in our minds with his later
namesake), as the literary politician impressing his
views upon a generation; we are offended by the
constant reminder of his scholarship. We forget the
comedy in the humours, and the serious artist in the
scholar. Jonson has suffered in public opinion, as
anyone must suffer who is forced to talk about his
art.

If you examine the first hundred lines or more of
Volpone the verse appears to be in the manner of
Marlowe, more deliberate, more mature, but without Marlowe's inspiration. It looks like mere
'rhetoric', certainly not 'deeds and language such as
men do use'. It appears to us, in fact, forced and
flagitious bombast. That it is not 'rhetoric', or at
least not vicious rhetoric, we do not know until we

are able to review the whole play. For the consistent maintenance of this manner conveys in the end an effect not of verbosity, but of bold, even shocking and terrifying directness. We have difficulty in saying exactly what produces this simple and single effect. It is not in any ordinary way due to management of intrigue. Jonson employs immense dramatic constructive skill: it is not so much skill in plot as skill in doing without a plot. He never manipulates as complicated a plot as that of *The Merchant of Venice*; he has in his best plays nothing like the intrigue of Restoration comedy. In *Bartholomew Fair* it is hardly a plot at all; the marvel of the play is the bewildering rapid chaotic action of the fair; it is the fair itself, not anything that happens in the fair. In *Volpone,* or *The Alchemist,* or *The Silent Woman,* the plot is enough to keep the players in motion; it is rather an 'action' than a plot. The plot does not hold the play together; what holds the play together is a unity of inspiration that radiates into plot and personages alike.

We have attempted to make more precise the sense in which it was said that Jonson's work is 'of the surface'; carefully avoiding the word 'superficial'. For there is work contemporary with Jonson's which is superficial in a pejorative sense in which the word cannot be applied to Jonson—the work of Beaumont and Fletcher. If we look at the work of Jonson's great contemporaries, Shakespeare, and also Donne and Webster and Tourneur (and sometimes Middleton), have a depth, a third dimension, as Mr. Gregory Smith rightly calls it, which Jonson's work has not. Their words have often a network of tentacular roots reaching down to the deepest terrors and desires. Jonson's most certainly have not; but in Beaumont and Fletcher we may think that at times we find it. Looking closer, we discover that the blossoms of Beaumont and Fletcher's imagination draw no sustenance from the soil, but are cut and slightly withered flowers stuck into sand.

Wilt thou, hereafter, when they talk of me,
As thou shalt hear nothing but infamy,
Remember some of these things? . . .
I pray thee, do; for thou shalt never see me so again.

Hair woven in many a curious warp,
Able in endless error to enfold
The wandering soul. . . .

Detached from its context, this looks like the verse of the greater poets; just as lines of Jonson, detached from their context, look like inflated or empty fustian. But the evocative quality of the verse of Beaumont and Fletcher depends upon a clever appeal to emotions and associations which they have not themselves grasped; it is hollow. It is superficial with

a vacuum behind it; the superficies of Jonson is solid.
It is what it is; it does not pretend to be another
thing. But it is so very conscious and deliberate that
we must look with eyes alert to the whole before
we apprehend the significance of any part. We cannot call a man's work superficial when it is the creation of a world; a man cannot be accused of dealing
superficially with the world which he himself has
created; the superficies *is* the world. Jonson's characters conform to the logic of the emotions of their
world. They are not fancy, because they have a
logic of their own; and this logic illuminates the
actual world, because it gives us a new point of
view from which to inspect it.

A writer of power and intelligence, Jonson endeavoured to promulgate, as a formula and pro-
gramme of reform, what he chose to do himself;
and he not unnaturally laid down in abstract theory
what is in reality a personal point of view. And it is
in the end of no value to discuss Jonson's theory and
practice unless we recognize and seize this point of
view, which escapes the formulæ, and which is what
makes his plays worth reading. Jonson behaved as
the great creative mind that he was: he created his
own world, a world from which his followers, as
well as the dramatists who were trying to do something wholly different, are excluded. Remembering
this, we turn to Mr. Gregory Smith's objection—

that Jonson's characters lack the third dimension, have no life out of the theatrical existence in which they appear—and demand an inquest. The objection implies that the characters are purely the work of intellect, or the result of superficial observation of a world which is faded or mildewed. It implies that the characters are lifeless. But if we dig beneath the theory, beneath the observation, beneath the deliberate drawing and the theatrical and dramatic elaboration, there is discovered a kind of power, animating Volpone, Busy, Fitzdottrel, the literary ladies of *Epicœne*, even Bobadil, which comes from below the intellect, and for which no theory of humours will account. And it is the same kind of power which vivifies Trimalchio, and Panurge, and some but not all of the 'comic' characters of Dickens. The fictive life of this kind is not to be circumscribed by a reference to 'comedy' or to 'farce'; it is not exactly the kind of life which informs the characters of Molière or that which informs those of Marivaux—two writers who were, besides, doing something quite different the one from the other. But it is something which distinguishes Barabas from Shylock, Epicure Mammon from Falstaff, Faustus from—if you will—Macbeth; Marlowe and Jonson from Shakespeare and the Shakespearians, Webster, and Tourneur. It is not merely Humours: for neither Volpone nor Mosca is a humour. No theory of humours could

account for Jonson's best plays or the best characters
in them. We want to know at what point the comedy of humours passes into a work of art, and why
Jonson is not Brome.

The creation of a work of art, we will say the
creation of a character in a drama, consists in the
process of transfusion of the personality, or, in a
deeper sense, the life, of the author into the character. This is a very different matter from the ortho-
dox creation in one's own image. The ways in which
the passions and desires of the creator may be satis-
fied in the work of art are complex and devious. In
a painter they may take the form of a predilection
for certain colours, tones, or lightings; in a writer
the original impulse may be even more strangely
transmuted. Now, we may say with Mr. Gregory
Smith that Falstaff or a score of Shakespeare's characters have a 'third dimension' that Jonson's have
not. This will mean, not that Shakespeare's spring
from the feelings or imagination and Jonson's from
the intellect or invention; they have equally an emotional source; but that Shakespeare's represent a
more complex tissue of feelings and desires, as well
as a more supple, a more susceptible temperament.
Falstaff is not only the roast Manningtree ox with
the pudding in his belly; he also 'grows old', and,
finally, his nose is as sharp as a pen. He was perhaps
the *satisfaction* of more, and of more complicated

F   81

feelings; and perhaps he was, as the great tragic characters must have been, the offspring of deeper, less apprehensible feelings: deeper, but not necessarily stronger or more intense, than those of Jonson. It is obvious that the spring of the difference is not the difference between feeling and thought, or superior insight, superior perception, on the part of Shakespeare, but his susceptibility to a greater range of emotion, and emotion deeper and more obscure. But his characters are no more 'alive' than are the characters of Jonson.

The world they live in is a larger one. But small worlds—the worlds which artists create—do not differ only in magnitude; if they are complete worlds, drawn to scale in every part, they differ in kind also. And Jonson's world has this scale. His type of personality found its relief in something falling under the category of burlesque or farce—though when you are dealing with a *unique* world, like his, these terms fail to appease the desire for definition. It is not, at all events, the farce of Molière: the latter is more analytic, more an intellectual redistribution. It is not defined by the word 'satire'. Jonson poses as a satirist. But satire like Jonson's is great in the end not by hitting off its object, but by creating it; the satire is merely the means which leads to the æsthetic result, the impulse which projects a new world into a new orbit. In *Every Man in his Humour* there is a neat, a very neat, comedy of humours. In discovering and proclaiming in this play the new genre Jonson was simply recognizing, unconsciously, the route which opened out in the proper direction for his instincts. His characters are and remain, like Marlowe's, simplified characters; but the simplification does not consist in the dominance of a particular humour or monomania. That is a very superficial account of it. The simplification consists largely in reduction of detail, in the seizing of aspects relevant to the relief of an emotional impulse which remains the same for that character, in making the character conform to a particular setting. This stripping is essential to the art, to which is also essential a flat distortion in the drawing; it is an art of caricature, of great caricature, like Marlowe's. It is a great caricature, which is beautiful; and a great humour, which is serious. The 'world' of Jonson is sufficiently large; it is a world of poetic imagination; it is sombre. He did not get the third dimension, but he was not trying to get it.

If we approach Jonson with less frozen awe of his learning, with a clearer understanding of his 'rhetoric' and its applications, if we grasp the fact that the knowledge required of the reader is not archæology but knowledge of Jonson, we can derive not only instruction in two-dimensional life—but enjoyment. We can even apply him, be aware of him as a part of our literary inheritance craving further expression. Of all the dramatists of his time, Jonson is probably the one whom the present age would find the most sympathetic, if it knew him. There is a brutality, a lack of sentiment, a polished surface, a handling of large bold designs in brilliant colours, which ought to attract about three thousand people in London and elsewhere. At least, if we had a contemporary Shakespeare and a contemporary Jonson, it might be the Jonson who would arouse the enthusiasm of the intelligentsia. Though he is saturated in literature, he never sacrifices the theatrical qualities—theatrical in the most favourable sense—to literature or to the study of character. His work is a titanic show. Jonson's masques, an important part of his work, are neglected; our flaccid culture lets shows and literature fade, but prefers faded literature to faded shows. There are hundreds of people who have read *Comus* to ten who have read the *Masque of Blackness*. *Comus* contains fine poetry, and poetry exemplifying some merits to which Jonson's masque poetry cannot pretend. Nevertheless, *Comus* is the death of the masque; it is the transition of a form of art—even of a form which existed for but a short generation—into 'literature', literature cast in a form which has lost its application. Even though *Comus* was a masque at Ludlow Castle, Jonson had, what Milton came perhaps too late to have, a sense for the living art; his art was applied. The masques can still be read, and with pleasure, by anyone who will take the trouble—a trouble which in this part of Jonson is, indeed, a study of antiquities—to imagine them in action, displayed with the music, costumes, dances, and the scenery of Inigo Jones. They are additional evidence that Jonson had a fine sense of form, of the purpose for which a particular form is intended; evidence that he was a literary artist even more than he was a man of letters.

THOMAS MIDDLETON

Thomas Middleton, the dramatic writer, was not very highly thought of in his own time; the date of his death is not known; we know only that he was buried on July 4th, 1627. He was one of the most voluminous, and one of the best, dramatic writers of his time. But it is easy to understand why he is not better known or more popular. It is difficult to imagine his 'personality'. Several new personalities have recently been fitted to the name of Shakespeare; Jonson is a real figure—our imagination plays about him discoursing at the Mermaid, or laying down the law to Drummond of Hawthornden; Chapman has become a breezy British character as firm as Nelson or Wellington; Webster and Donne are real people for the more intellectual; even Tourneur (Churton Collins having said the last word about him) is a 'personality'. But Middleton, who collaborated shamelessly, who is hardly separated from Rowley, Middleton, who wrote plays so diverse as *Women Beware Women* and *A Game at Chess* and *The Roaring Girl*, Middleton remains merely a collective name for a number of plays—some of which, like *The Spanish Gypsy*, are patently by other people.[1]

If we write about Middleton's plays we must write about Middleton's plays, and not about Middleton's personality. Many of these plays are still in doubt. Of all the Elizabethan dramatists Middleton seems the most impersonal, the most indifferent to personal fame or perpetuity, the readiest, except Rowley, to accept collaboration. Also he is the most various. His greatest tragedies and his greatest comedies are as if written by two different men. Yet there seems no doubt that Middleton was both a great comic writer and a great tragic writer. There are a sufficient number of plays, both tragedies and comedies, in which his hand is so far unquestioned, to establish his greatness. His greatness is not that of a peculiar personality, but of a great artist or artisan of the Elizabethan epoch. We have among others *The Changeling*, *Women Beware Women*, and *A Game at Chess*; and we have *The Roaring Girl* and *A Trick to Catch the Old One*. And that is enough. Between the tragedies and the comedies of Shakespeare, and certainly between the tragedies and the

[1] Mr. Dugdale Sykes has written authoritatively on this subject.

comedies of Jonson, we can establish a relation; we can see, for Shakespeare or Jonson, that each had in the end a personal point of view which can be called neither comic nor tragic. But with Middleton we can establish no such relation. He remains merely a name, a voice, the author of certain plays, which are all of them great plays. He has no point of view, is neither sentimental nor cynical; he is neither resigned, nor disillusioned, nor romantic; he has no message. He is merely the name which associates six or seven great plays.

For there is no doubt about *The Changeling*. Like all of the plays attributed to Middleton, it is long-winded and tiresome; the characters talk too much, and then suddenly stop talking and act; they are real and impelled irresistibly by the fundamental motions of humanity to good or evil. This mixture of tedious discourse and sudden reality is everywhere in the work of Middleton, in his comedy also. In *The Roaring Girl* we read with toil through a mass of cheap conventional intrigue, and suddenly realize that we are, and have been for some time without knowing it, observing a real and unique human being. In reading *The Changeling* we may think, till almost the end of the play, that we have been concerned merely with a fantastic Elizabethan morality, and then discover that we are looking on at a dispassionate exposure of fundamental passions of any time and any place. The usual opinion remains the just judgment: *The Changeling* is Middleton's greatest play. The morality of the convention seems to us absurd. To many intelligent readers this play has only an historical interest, and serves only to illustrate the moral taboos of the Elizabethans. The heroine is a young woman who, in order to dispose of a fiancé to whom she is indifferent, so that she may marry the man she loves, accepts the offer of an adventurer to murder the affianced, at the price (as she finds in due course) of becoming the murderer's mistress. Such a plot is, to a modern mind, absurd; and the consequent tragedy seems a fuss about nothing. But *The Changeling* is not merely contingent for its effect upon our acceptance of Elizabethan good form or convention; it is, in fact, no more dependent upon the convention of its epoch than a play like *A Doll's House*. Underneath the convention there is the stratum of truth permanent in human nature. The tragedy of *The Changeling* is an eternal tragedy, as permanent as *Œdipus* or *Antony and Cleopatra*; it is the tragedy of the not naturally bad but irresponsible and undeveloped nature, caught in the consequences of its own action. In every age and in every civilization there are instances of the same thing: the unmoral nature, suddenly trapped in the inexorable toils of morality—of morality not made by man but by Nature—and forced to take the consequences of an act which it had planned light-heartedly. Beatrice is not a moral creature; she becomes moral only by becoming damned. Our conventions are not the same as those which Middleton assumed for his play. But the possibility of that frightful discovery of morality remains permanent.

The words in which Middleton expresses his tragedy are as great as the tragedy. The process through which Beatrice, having decided that De Flores is the instrument for her purpose, passes from aversion to habituation, remains a permanent commentary on human nature. The directness and precision of De Flores are masterly, as is also the virtuousness of Beatrice on first realizing his motives—

> *Why, 'tis impossible thou canst be so wicked,*
> *Or shelter such a cunning cruelty,*
> *To make his death the murderer of my honour!*
> *Thy language is so bold and vicious,*
> *I cannot see which way I can forgive it*
> *With any modesty*

—a passage which ends with the really great lines of De Flores, lines of which Shakespeare or Sophocles might have been proud:

> *Can you weep Fate from its determined purpose?*
> *So soon may you weep me.*

But what constitutes the essence of the tragedy is something which has not been sufficiently remarked; it is the *habituation* of Beatrice to her sin; it becomes no longer merely sin but custom. Such is the essence of the tragedy of *Macbeth*—the habituation to crime. And in the end Beatrice, having been so long the enforced conspirator of De Flores, becomes (and this is permanently true to human nature) more *his* partner, *his* mate, than the mate and partner of the man for the love of whom she consented to the crime. Her lover disappears not only from the scene but from her own imagination. When she says of De Flores,

A wondrous necessary man, my lord,

her praise is more than half sincere; and at the end she belongs far more to De Flores—towards whom, at the beginning, she felt strong physical repulsion—than to her lover Alsemero. It is De Flores, in the end, to whom she belongs as Francesca to Paolo:

Beneath the stars, upon yon meteor
Ever hung my fate, 'mongst things corruptible;
I ne'er could pluck it from him; my loathing
Was prophet to the rest, but ne'er believed.

And De Flores's cry is perfectly sincere and in character:

I loved this woman in spite of her heart;
Her love I earned out of Piracquo's murder . . .
Yes, and her honour's prize
Was my reward; I thank life for nothing
But that pleasure; it was so sweet to me,
That I have drunk up all, left none behind
For any man to pledge me.

The tragedy of Beatrice is not that she has lost Alsemero, for whose possession she played; it is that she has won De Flores. Such tragedies are not limited to Elizabethan times: they happen every day and perpetually. The greatest tragedies are occupied with great and permanent moral conflicts: the great tragedies of Æschylus, of Sophocles, of Corneille, of Racine, of Shakespeare have the same burden. In poetry, in dramatic technique, *The Changeling* is inferior to the best plays of Webster. But in the moral essence of tragedy it is safe to say that in this play Middleton is surpassed by one Elizabethan alone, and that is Shakespeare. In some respects in which Elizabethan tragedy can be compared to French or to Greek tragedy *The Changeling* stands above every tragic play of its time, except those of Shakespeare.

The genius which blazed in *The Changeling* was fitful but not accidental. The best tragedy after *The Changeling* is *Women Beware Women*. The thesis of

93

the play, as the title indicates, is more arbitrary and less fundamental. The play itself, although less disfigured by ribaldry or clowning, is more tedious. Middleton sinks himself in conventional moralizing of the epoch; so that, if we are impatient, we decide that he gives merely a document of Elizabethan humbug—and then suddenly a personage will blaze out in genuine fire of vituperation. The wickedness of the personages in *Women Beware Women* is conventional wickedness of the stage of the time; yet slowly the exasperation of Bianca, the wife who married beneath her, beneath the ambitions to which she was entitled, emerges from the negative; slowly the real human passions emerge from the mesh of interest in which they begin. And here again Middleton, in writing what appears on the surface a conventional picture-palace Italian melodrama of the time, has caught permanent human feelings. And in this play Middleton shows his interest—more than any of his contemporaries—in innuendo and double meanings; and makes use of that game of chess, which he was to use more openly and directly for satire in that perfect piece of literary political art, *A Game at Chess*. The irony could not be improved upon:

Did I not say my duke would fetch you o'er, Widow?
I think you spoke in earnest when you said it, madam.

94

And my black king makes all the haste he can too.
Well, madam, we may meet with him in time yet.
I've given thee blind mate twice.

There is hardly anything truer in Elizabethan drama than Bianca's gradual self-will and self-importance in consequence of her courtship by the duke:

Troth, you speak wondrous well for your old house
 here;
'Twill shortly fall down at your feet to thank you,
Or stoop, when you go to bed, like a good child,
To ask you blessing.

In spite of all the long-winded speeches, in spite of all the conventional Italianate horrors, Bianca remains, like Beatrice in *The Changeling*, a real woman; as real, indeed, as any woman of Elizabethan tragedy. Bianca is a woman of the type who is purely moved by vanity.

But if Middleton understood woman in tragedy better than any of the Elizabethans—better than the creator of the Duchess of Malfy, better than Marlowe, better than Tourneur, or Shirley, or Fletcher, better than any of them except Shakespeare alone— he was also able, in his comedy, to present a finer woman than any of them. *The Roaring Girl* has no apparent relation to Middleton's tragedies, yet it is agreed to be primarily the work of Middleton. It is typical of the comedies of Middleton, and it is the best. In his tragedies Middleton employs all the Italianate horrors of his time, and obviously for the purpose of pleasing the taste of his time; yet underneath we feel always a quiet and undisturbed vision of things as they are and not 'another thing'. So in his comedies. The comedies are long-winded; the fathers are heavy fathers, and rant as heavy fathers should; the sons are wild and wanton sons, and perform all the pranks to be expected of them; the machinery is the usual Elizabethan machinery; Middleton is solicitous to please his audience with what they expect; but there is underneath the same steady impersonal passionless observation of human nature. *The Roaring Girl* is as artificial as any comedy of the time; its plot creaks loudly; yet the Girl herself is always real. She may rant, she may behave preposterously, but she remains a type of the sort of woman who has renounced all happiness for herself and who lives only for a principle. Nowhere more clearly than in *The Roaring Girl* can the hand of Middleton be distinguished from the hand of Dekker. Dekker is all sentiment; and, indeed, in the so admired passages of *A Fair Quarrel*, applauded by Lamb, the mood if not the hand of Dekker seems to the unexpert critic to be more present than Middleton's. *A Fair Quarrel* seems as much, if not more, Dekker's than Middleton's. Similarly with *The*

Spanish Gypsy, which can with difficulty be attributed to Middleton. But the feeling about Moll Cut-Purse of *The Roaring Girl* is Middleton's rather than anybody's. In Middleton's tragedy there is a strain of realism underneath, which is one with the poetry; and in his comedy we find the same thing.

In her recent book on *The Social Mode of Restoration Comedy,* Miss Kathleen Lynch calls attention to the gradual transition from Elizabethan-Jacobean to Restoration comedy. She observes, what is certainly true, that Middleton is the greatest 'realist' in Jacobean comedy. Miss Lynch's extremely suggestive thesis is that the transition from Elizabethan-Jacobean to later Caroline comedy is primarily economic: that the interest changes from the citizen aping gentry to the citizen become gentry and accepting that code of manners. In the comedy of Middleton certainly there is as yet no code of manners; but the merchant of Cheapside is *aiming* at becoming a member of the county gentry. Miss Lynch remarks: 'Middleton's keen concentration on the spectacle of the interplay of different social classes marks an important development in realistic comedy.' She calls attention to this aspect of Middleton's comedy, that it marks, better than the romantic comedy of Shakespeare, or the comedy of Jonson, occupied with what Jonson thought to be permanent and not transient aspects of human nature, the transition between the aristocratic world which preceded the Tudors and the plutocratic modern world which the Tudors initiated and encouraged. By the time of the return of Charles II, as Miss Lynch points out, society had been reorganized and formed, and social conventions had been created. In the Tudor times birth still counted (though nearly all the great families were extinct); by the time of Charles II only breeding counted. The comedy of Middleton, and the comedy of Brome, and the comedy of Shirley, is intermediate, as Miss Lynch remarks. Middleton, she observes, marks the transitional stage in which the London tradesman was anxious to cease to be a tradesman and to become a country gentleman. The words of his City Magnate in *Michaelmas Terme* had not yet lost their point:

'A fine journey in the Whitsun holydays, i' faith, to ride with a number of citizens and their wives, some upon pillions, some upon side-saddles, I and little Thomasine i' the middle, our son and heir, Sim Quomodo, in a peach-colour taffeta jacket, some horse length, or a long yard before us—there will be a fine show on's I can tell you.'

But Middleton's comedy is not, like the comedy of Congreve, the comedy of a set social behaviour; it is still, like the later comedy of Dickens, the comedy of individuals, in spite of the continual

motions of city merchants towards county gentility.
In the comedy of the Restoration a figure such as
that of Moll Cut-Purse would have been impossible.
As a social document the comedy of Middleton
illustrates the transition from government by a
landed aristocracy to government by a city aristocracy gradually engrossing the land. As such it is of
the greatest interest. But as literature, as a dispassionate picture of human nature, Middleton's comedy
deserves to be remembered chiefly by its real—perpetually real—and human figure of Moll the Roaring Girl. That Middleton's comedy was 'photographic', that it introduces us to the low life of the
time far better than anything in the comedy of
Shakespeare or the comedy of Jonson, better than
anything except the pamphlets of Dekker and Greene
and Nashe, there is little doubt. But it produced one
great play—*The Roaring Girl*—a great play in spite
of the tedious long speeches of some of the principal
characters, in spite of the clumsy machinery of the
plot: for the reason that Middleton was a great
observer of human nature, without fear, without
sentiment, without prejudice.

And Middleton in the end—after criticism has sub-
tracted all that Rowley, all that Dekker, all that
others contributed—is a great example of great
English drama. He has no message; he is merely a
great recorder. Incidentally, in flashes and when the

dramatic need comes, he is a great poet, a great master of versification:

> *I that am of your blood was taken from you*
> *For your better health; look no more upon't,*
> *But cast it to the ground regardlessly,*
> *Let the common sewer take it from distinction.*
> *Beneath the stars, upon yon meteor*
> *Ever hung my fate, 'mongst things corruptible;*
> *I ne'er could pluck it from him; my loathing*
> *Was prophet to the rest, but ne'er believed.*

The man who wrote these lines remains inscrutable, solitary, unadmired; welcoming collaboration, indifferent to fame; dying no one knows when and no one knows how; attracting, in three hundred years, no personal admiration. Yet he wrote one tragedy which more than any play except those of Shakespeare has a profound and permanent moral value and horror; and one comedy which more than any Elizabethan comedy realizes a free and noble womanhood.

THOMAS HEYWOOD

There are a few of the Elizabethan dramatists, notably Marlowe and Ben Jonson, who always return to our minds with the reality of personal acquaintances. We know them unmistakably through their own writings—Jonson partly through his conversations with Drummond—and by a few anecdotes of the kind which, even when apocryphal, remain as evidence of the personal impression that such men must have made upon their contemporaries. There are others whom we can remember only by the association of their names with a play, or a group of plays. Of all these men Thomas Heywood is one of the dimmest figures; and it is interesting to remark how very dim he still remains even after Dr. Clark's exhaustive industry.[1] Dr. Clark appears to have discovered and assembled all the information that we can ever expect to have;

[1] *Thomas Heywood: Playwright and Miscellanist,* by A. M. Clark. Oxford: Blackwell. 1931.

and it is certainly not his fault that Heywood makes still but a faint impression; in fact, Dr. Clark's book can help us considerably to understand why this is so. The book is solidly documentary; it is not, like some biographical essays with scanty material, stuffed out with appreciation and conjecture. It is, in fact, an admirable account of the life of a typical literary Jack-of-all-trades of the epoch; the summary of Heywood's activities as a pamphleteer, with his works of what may be termed popular theology in the Puritan cause, is full of interest for anyone who cares about this lively and, in some respects, very remote age. And the book confirms the impression that Heywood—whom Dr. Clark shows convincingly to have been a Heywood of Mottram, in Cheshire, and not of the family of Heywood of Lincolnshire, the county of his birth—was a facile and sometimes felicitous purveyor of goods to the popular taste.

Heywood's reputation, which we owe primarily to Lamb and Hazlitt, is founded on *A Woman Killed with Kindness*; but *The English Traveller* and *The Wise Woman of Hogsdon* are not far below it; and the first part of *The Fair Maid of the West*, when it has been performed—twice, we believe, in recent years—was revealed as a rollicking piece of popular patriotic sentiment. Before considering whether this output has enough coherence to be treated with the dignity of an *œuvre*, there are several interesting attributions of Dr. Clark's which demand attention. The first and most important is *Appius and Virginia*.

The date of this play, which has long been a difficulty to students of Webster—a play far below Webster's best work, and in some respects dissimilar to it—forms one of Dr. Clark's reasons for attributing the play primarily to Heywood. This was, of course, the guess of Rupert Brooke; but, given the initial doubt which strikes any admirer of Webster, the opinion, when it comes from a close student of Heywood, has much stronger authority. Dr. Clark, however, is not content to take issue only with Mr. Sykes (who gives the whole play to Webster), though that is a serious task in itself. He dismisses, with hardly more attention than a few footnotes, the moderate and so far, we believe, impregnable view of Mr. F. L. Lucas. He refers, certainly, to Mr. Lucas's 'attempt to depreciate Heywood' as 'uncritical'; because Mr. Lucas, in his introduction to the play in his complete edition of Webster, doubts whether Heywood

'could have produced unaided so well-planned and reasonable a play. For there is a peculiar oafish simplicity about him which made him unable ever to create a single piece, except perhaps *Edward IV*, which is not deformed by pages of utter drivel.'

Mr. Lucas has perhaps written with a heat uncommon among Elizabethan scholars, though refreshing; yet his doubt whether Heywood could have planned the play is one likely to strike anyone who reads both Webster and Heywood without prejudices. To such a reader, the fact that Heywood is the author of *The Rape of Lucrece* strains credulity to the breaking point. But this, indeed, is the whole issue between Dr. Clark and Mr. Lucas. Neither doubts that both Heywood and Webster had a hand in the play; neither makes a claim for any third author. Dr. Clark concludes that Heywood wrote the play and that 'at an unknown date Webster revised the play somewhat carelessly'. Mr. Lucas can more easily believe that Webster wrote, or designed and partly wrote, the play, and that Heywood either revised or completed it. We are left with a narrow choice and a fine distinction; in fact, we are left to our personal impressions. The feeling of the present reviewer, at least, is that the structure of the play is more credibly assignable to Webster, as well as the good lines which nobody denies him.

Our inclination to this conclusion is confirmed, if anything, by Dr. Clark's theory of Heywood's hand in *The Jew of Malta*. It seems to us that here Dr. Clark's scholarly theory is really founded upon a critical presupposition. He holds a not uncommon view that 'so far as [Marlowe's] conception of Barabas is concerned, the play might finish with the second act'. But he adds, 'so far as we know Marlowe invented the plot', which is a considerable concession; and also admits that there is a very little in Acts III, IV and V which Marlowe may have written. He says, 'in the play we probably still have the main incidents as originally determined, but now crowded mostly into V to make room for certain ribaldry and gruesome farce'. There is perhaps a little ribaldry which we should prefer not to attribute to Marlowe, and of a kind of which Heywood was certainly capable; but the most 'gruesome farce' is found in Act IV, Scenes i and ii; which the mere critic may maintain to be farce of a gruesomeness a cut above Heywood, and by no means unworthy of Marlowe. That the latter part of the play is garbled, few would doubt; that the writer who filled in the remains of Marlowe's play was Heywood, Dr. Clark makes out a good case; but mutilated and patched as the play probably is, we may still see in it a conception of Barabas which is by no means finished with the second act.

The third of Dr. Clark's interesting ascriptions concerns *A Yorkshire Tragedy*. This abrupt little play has been somewhat overrated, singularly so by Swinburne. Dr. Clark's association of it with *The Miseries of Enforced Marriage*, and his explanation of its inconsistencies through this association, is an excellent piece of reasoning. So far as the verse is concerned, most of it is not too bad to be Heywood's, and the best line and a half——

But you are playing in the angels' laps
And will not look on me——

strike us as a *trouvaille* which might have been possible to Heywood. The best of the play is the part of the 'little son':

'What, ail you, Father? are you not well? I cannot scourge my top as long as you stand so: you take up all the room with your wide legs. Puh, you cannot make me afeard with this; I fear no vizards, nor bugbears'

and as we cannot allege any other minor dramatist as more competent to have written this touching dialogue than Heywood, we are hardly in a strong position to refuse it to him. This then, we think, is the most valuable of Dr. Clark's ascriptions.

None of these attributions, interesting as is the last of them in itself, can make very much difference to our estimate of Heywood as a dramatist and a poet; and it is upon the indisputable plays that we found our opinion of him. These indisputable plays exhibit what may be called the minimum degree of unity. Similar subject-matter and treatment appear in several; the same stage skill, the same versifying ability. The sensibility is merely that of ordinary people in ordinary life—which is the reason, perhaps, why Heywood is misleadingly called a 'realist'. Behind the motions of his personages, the shadows of the human world, there is no reality of moral synthesis; to inform the verse there is no vision, none of the artist's power to give undefinable unity to the most various material. In the work of nearly all of those of his contemporaries who are as well known as he there is at least some inchoate pattern; there is, as it would often be called, personality. Of those of Heywood's plays which are worth reading, each is worth reading for itself, but none throws any illumination upon any other.

Heywood's versification is never on a very high poetic level, but at its best is often on a high dramatic level. This can be illustrated by one of the best known of quotations from *A Woman Killed with Kindness*:

> *O speak no more!*
> *For more than this I know, and have recorded*
> *Within the red-leaved table of my heart.*
> *Fair, and of all beloved, I was not fearful*
> *Bluntly to give my life into your hand,*
> *And at one hazard all my earthly means.*
> *Go, tell your husband; he will turn me off,*
> *And I am then undone. I care not, I;*
> *'Twas for your sake. Perchance in rage he'll kill me,*

I care not, 'twas for you. Say I incur
The general name of villain through the world,
Of traitor to my friend; I care not, I.
Beggary, shame, death, scandal, and reproach,
For you I'll hazard all: why, what care I?
For you I'll live, and in your love I'll die.

The image at the beginning of this passage does not, it is true, deserve its fame. 'Table of my heart' is a legitimate, though hardly striking, metaphor; but to call it *red-leaved* is to press the anatomical aspect into a ridiculous figure. It is not a conceit, as when Crashaw deliberately telescopes one image into another, but merely the irreflective grasping after a fine trope. But in the lines that follow the most skilful use is made of regular blank verse to emphasize the argument; and it is, even to the judicious couplet at the end, a speech which any actor should be happy to declaim. The speech is perfect for the situation; the most persuasive that Wendoll could have made to Mrs. Frankford; and it persuades us into accepting her surrender. And this instance of verse which is only moderately poetical but very highly dramatic is by no means singular in Heywood's work.

And undeniably Heywood was not without skill in the construction of plays. It is unreasonable to complain of *A Woman Killed with Kindness* that it is improbable that a woman who has lived very hap-

pily with her husband and borne children should
suddenly and easily be seduced by a man who had
been living in the house the whole time; we consider that the seduction is made extremely plausible.
What is perhaps clumsy is the beginning superflu-
ously by a scene directly after the marriage of the
Frankfords, instead of by a scene marking the happiness of the pair up to the moment of Wendoll's
declaration. Sufficient verisimilitude is maintained to
the end; we accept the Elizabethan convention of
very quick death from heartbreak; and the last scene
is really affecting. It is true that Mistress Frankford's
words:

Out of my zeal to Heaven, whither now I'm bound,

seem to rely upon some curiously unorthodox theology; and even if death from broken heart secures
the remission of sins, it hardly became Mrs. Frankford to be so certain of it. But such a moral sentiment is perhaps not unique in the ethics of Elizabethan drama; and other small touches in the play,
such as the finding of the guitar, well deserve the
praise they have received. It is in the underplot, as
in some other plays, that Heywood is least skilful.
This theme—a man ready to prostitute his sister as
payment for a debt of honour—is too grotesque
even to horrify us; but it is too obviously there
merely because an underplot is required to fill out

the play for us to feel anything but boredom when it recurs. Middleton's *The Changeling*, in every other respect a far finer play, must share with *A Woman Killed with Kindness* the discredit of having the weakest underplot of any important play in the whole Elizabethan repertory.

Indeed, Heywood suffers from one great handicap in attempting to write underplots at all—he was gifted with very little sense of humour, and therefore could not fall back upon the comic for the purpose. In attempting to be amusing he sometimes has recourse, as other men than harried playwrights have been known to do, to the lowest bawdiness, which leaves us less with a sense of repugnance for the man who could write it than with a sense of pity for the man who could think of nothing better. Here and there, in *The Wise Woman of Hogsdon* for instance, he succeeds with something not too far below Jonson to be comparable to that master's work; the wise woman herself, and her scenes with her clientèle, are capitally done, and earn for Heywood the title of 'realist' if any part of his work can. The scene of the unmasking of Young Chartley must be excellent fun when played. The underplot of *The English Traveller*, on the other hand, is a clumsy failure to do that in which only Jonson could have succeeded. But Heywood has no imaginative humour; and as he has so often been spoken of in the same breath with Dekker, that is a comparison which may justly be made. Just as Bess, the Fair Maid of the West, is a purely melodramatic figure beside the heroine of *The Roaring Girl*, so Heywood could no more have created the character of Cuddie Banks, in *The Witch*, than he could have written the magnificent tirade (a tirade which, if anything can, goes to prove that Middleton wrote *The Revenger's Tragedy*) which Middleton puts into the mouth of the chief character in the same play. Cuddie Banks, loving the dog whom he knows to be a devil, but loving him as dog while reproving him as devil, is worthy to rank with clowns of Shakespeare; he is not 'realistic', he is true.

It was in *The English Traveller* that Heywood found his best plot. Possibly the elder critics disapproved of the heroine's plighting herself to marry her admirer as soon as her elderly husband should die; but it is far less offensive to modern taste than many other situations in Elizabethan drama, and it is one which a modern novelist—not perhaps a quite modern novelist, but a Stendhal—might have made the most of. It is indeed a plot especially modern among Elizabethan plots; for the refinement of agony of the virtuous lover who has controlled his passion and then discovers that his lady has deceived both her husband, who is his friend, and himself, is really more poignant than the torment of the be-

trayed husband Frankford. The strange situation
à quatre, Master Wincott and his wife, young Geraldine and his faithless companion Delavil—and old
Geraldine neatly worked into the pattern as well—is
not only well thought of but well thought out; and
it is delicately phrased:

Y. GER.

> *Your husband's old, to whom my soul doth wish*
> *A Nestor's age, so much he merits from me;*
> *Yet if (as proof and Nature daily teach*
> *Men cannot always live, especially*
> *Such as are old and crazed) he be called hence,*
> *Fairly, in full maturity of time,*
> *And we two be reserved to after life,*
> *Will you confer your widowhood on me?*

WIFE.

> *You ask the thing I was about to beg;*
> *Your tongue hath spoke mine own thoughts. . . .*
> *Till that day come, you shall reserve yourself*
> *A single man; converse nor company*
> *With any woman, contract nor combine*
> *With maid or widow; which expected hour*
> *As I do wish not haste, so when it happens*
> *It shall not come unwelcome. You hear all;*
> *Vow this.*

Y. GER.

> *By all that you have said, I swear,*
> *And by this kiss confirm.*

WIFE.

> *You're now my brother;*
> *But then, my second husband.*

It could not have been done better. As in the passage from *A Woman Killed with Kindness* quoted above, the verse, which nowhere bursts into a flame of poetry, is yet economical and tidy, and formed to extract all the dramatic value possible from the situation. And it is by his refinement of sentiment, by his sympathetic delicacy in these two plays that Heywood deserves, and well deserves, to be remembered; for here he has accomplished what none of his contemporaries succeeded in accomplishing.

Yet we must concede that the interest is always sentimental, and never ethical. One has seen plays in our time which are just the sort of thing that Heywood would have written had he been our contemporary. It is usual for inferior authors at any time to accept whatever morality is current, because they are interested not to analyse the ethics but to exploit the sentiment. Mrs. Frankford yields to her seducer with hardly a struggle, and her decline and death are a tribute to popular sentiment; not, certainly, a vindication of inexorable moral law. She is in the sentimental tradition which peopled a period of nineteenth-century fiction with Little Em'lys; and which, if it now produces a generation of rather robuster heroines, has yet made no moral advance, because it has no vital relation to morals at all. For a Corneille or a Racine, the centre of interest in the situation of Mrs. Frankford or Mrs. Wincott would have been the moral conflict leading up to the fall; and even the absence of conflict, as in the seduction of Mathilde (if seduction it can be called) in *Le Rouge et le Noir*, can be treated by a moralist. The capital distinction is that between representation of human actions which have moral reality and representation of such as have only sentimental reality; and beside this, any distinction between 'healthy' and 'morbid' sentiment is trivial. It is well enough to speak of Heywood, as does Dr. Clark, as 'a man of tender charity . . . ever kindly to the fallen and with a gift of homely pathos and simple poetry'; though it does less than justice to Heywood to describe his pathos as 'homely' (for the famous pathos of 'Nan, Nan!' is no homelier than Lear's 'Never, never, never, never, never', though far below it). What matters is not whether Heywood was inspired by tender charity, but whether his actual productions are any more edifying, any more moral, than what Dr. Clark would call 'the slippery ethics' of Fletcher, Massinger and Ford.

The ethics of most of the greater Elizabethan dramatists is only intelligible as leading up to, or deriving from, that of Shakespeare: it has its significance, we mean, only in the light of Shakespeare's fuller revelation. There is another type of ethics, that of the satirist. In Shakespeare's work it is represented most nearly by *Timon* and *Troilus*, but in a mind with such prodigious capacity of development as Shakespeare's, the snarling vein could not endure. The kind of satire which is approached in *The Jew of Malta* reaches perhaps its highest point with *Volpone*; but it is a kind to which also approximates much of the work of Middleton and Tourneur, men who as writers must be counted morally higher than Fletcher or Ford or Heywood.

> *These by enchantments can whole lordships change*
> *To trunks of rich attire, turn ploughs and teams*
> *To Flanders mares and coaches, and huge trains*
> *Of servitors to a French butterfly.*
> *Have you not city-witches who can turn*
> *Their husbands' wares, whole standing shops of wares,*
> *To sumptuous tables, gardens of stolen sin;*
> *In one year wasting what scarce twenty win?*
> *Are not these witches?*

That dolorous aspect of human nature which in comedy is best portrayed by Molière, though Jonson and even Wycherley have the same burden, appears again and again in the tragic drama of Middleton and Tourneur. Without denying to Heywood what Dr. Clark attributes to him, a sense of 'the pity of it', we can find a profounder sense of the 'pity of it' in the lines quoted above which Middleton gives to the Witch of Edmonton. Heywood's sense of pity is genuine enough, but it is only the kind of pity that the ordinary playgoer, of any time, can appreciate. Heywood's is a drama of common life, not, in the highest sense, tragedy at all; there is no supernatural music from behind the wings. He would in any age have been a successful playwright; he is eminent in the pathetic, rather than the tragic. His nearest approach to those deeper emotions which shake the veil of Time is in that fine speech of Frankford which surely no men or women past their youth can read without a twinge of personal feeling:

> *O God! O God! that it were possible*
> *To undo things done; to call back yesterday. . . .*

CYRIL TOURNEUR

Although the tragedies which make immortal the name of Cyril Tourneur are accessible to everyone in the new Mermaid edition, it is still an event to have a new edition of the 'work' of this strange poet. Fifty-two years have passed since the edition in two volumes by Churton Collins. And this sumptuous critical edition of Professor Nicoll's[1] reminds us that it is time to revalue the work of Tourneur.

None of the Elizabethan dramatists is more puzzling; none offers less foothold for the scholarly investigator; and none is more dangerous for the literary critic. We know almost nothing of his life; we trace his hand in no collaboration. He has left only two plays; and it has been doubted even whether the same man wrote both; and if he did, as most

[1] *The Works of Cyril Tourneur.* Edited by Allardyce Nicoll. With decorations by Frederick Carter. London: The Fanfrolico Press.

scholars agree, there is still some doubt as to which he wrote first. Yet in no plays by any minor Elizabethan is a more positive personality revealed than in *The Revenger's Tragedy*. No Elizabethan dramatist offers greater temptation: to the scholar, to hazard conjecture of fact; and to the critic, to hazard conjecture of significance. We may be sure that what Mr. Nicoll does not know is unknown to anybody; and it is no disrespect to his scholarship and diligence to remark how little, in the fifty-two years of Elizabethan research since Collins, has been added to our knowledge of the singular poet with the delightful name. Churton Collins, in his admirable introduction, really knows nothing at all about the man's life; and all that later students have been able to do is to piece together several probable shreds. That there was a family of Tourneurs is certain; the precise place in it of Cyril is, as Mr. Nicoll freely admits, a matter of speculation. And, with all the plausible guesses possible, Mr. Nicoll tells us that Tourneur's 'whole early life is a complete blank'. What he does give us is good reason for believing that Tourneur, with perhaps other members of the family, was a servant of the Cecils; and he adds to our knowledge a prose piece, 'The Character of Robert Earl of Salisbury'. Besides the two tragedies, he also gives 'The Transformed Metamorphosis', the 'Funeral Poem upon the Death

of Sir Francis Vere', and the Elegy on the death of
Prince Henry, already canonically attributed to
Tourneur; and 'Laugh and Lie Down', a satirical
pamphlet, no better and no worse than dozens of
others, which is probably Tourneur's—at least, it is
attributed to him, and there is no particular reason
why he should not be the author.

The information of fifty years is meagre and
probably will never be improved. It is astonishingly
incongruous with what we feel we know about
Tourneur after reading the two plays: two plays as
different from all plays by known Elizabethans as
they are from each other. In Elizabethan drama, the
critic is rash who will assert boldly that any play is
by a single hand. But with each of these, *The
Atheist's Tragedy* and *The Revenger's Tragedy*, the
literary critic feels that, even were there some collaboration, one mind guided the whole work; and
feels that the mind was not that of one of the other
well-known dramatic writers. Certainly, Tourneur
has made a very deep impression upon the minds of
those critics who have admired him. It is to be re-
gretted, however, that Professor Nicoll, at the
beginning of his otherwise sober and just introduction, has quoted the hysterical phrase of Marcel
Schwob's *vie imaginaire* of Tourneur. To say that
Tourneur *naquit de l'union d'un dieu inconnu avec une
prostituée* is a pardonable excess of a romantic period,

a pardonable excess on the part of a poet discovering a foreign poet. But this is not criticism; and it is a misleading introduction to the work of a man who was a great English poet; and it produces an impression which is increased by the excellent but too *macabre* decorations of Mr. Carter. What matters first is the beauty of the verse and the unity of the dramatic pattern in the two plays.

The author of *The Atheist's Tragedy* and *The Revenger's Tragedy* belongs critically among the earlier of the followers of Shakespeare. If Ford and Shirley and Fletcher represent the decadence, and Webster the last ripeness, then Tourneur belongs a little earlier than Webster. He is nearer to Middleton, and has some affinity to that curious and still underestimated poet Marston. The difference between his mind and that of Webster is very great; if we assigned his plays to any other known dramatist, Webster would be the last choice. For Webster is a slow, deliberate, careful writer, very much the conscious artist. He was incapable of writing so badly or so tastelessly as Tourneur sometimes did, but he is never quite so surprising as Tourneur sometimes is. Moreover, Webster, in his greatest tragedies, has a kind of pity for *all* of his characters, an attitude towards good and bad alike which helps to unify the Webster pattern. Tourneur has no such feeling for any of his characters; and in this respect is nearer,

as Professor Stoll has pointed out and Professor
Nicoll has reminded us, to the author of *Antonio and
Mellida*. Of all his other contemporaries, Middleton
is the nearest. But Mr. Nicoll, we think quite rightly,
rejects Mr. E. H. C. Oliphant's theory that Middleton is the author of *The Revenger's Tragedy*, and with
Mr. Dugdale Sykes restores the play to Tourneur.
And, in spite of Mr. Oliphant's weight of proba-
bilities, there is one quality of Middleton which we
do not find in the two plays attributed to Tourneur.
The finest of the tragic characters of Middleton live
in a way which differs from Tourneur's, not in
degree but kind; and they have flashes of a kind of
satiric wit unknown to Tourneur, in whom wit is
supplied by a fierce grotesquerie. In reading one
play of Middleton, either *The Changeling* or *Women
Beware Women*, for instance, we can recognize an
author capable of considerable variety in his dramatic work; in reading either of Tourneur's plays we
recognize a narrow mind, capable at most of the
limited range of Marston.

Indeed, none of the characters of Tourneur, even
the notable Vindice, the protagonist of *The Revenger's Tragedy*, is by himself invested with much
humanity either for good or evil. But dramatic
characters may live in more than one way; and a
dramatist like Tourneur can compensate his defects
by the intensity of his virtues. Characters should be

real in relation to our own life, certainly, as even a very minor character of Shakespeare may be real; but they must also be real in relation to each other; and the closeness of emotional pattern in the latter way is an important part of dramatic merit. The personages of Tourneur have, like those of Marston, and perhaps in a higher degree, this togetherness. They may be distortions, grotesques, almost childish caricatures of humanity, but they are all distorted to scale. Hence the whole action, from their appearance to their ending, 'no common action' indeed, has its own self-subsistent reality. For closeness of texture, in fact, there are no plays beyond Shakespeare's, and the best of Marlowe and Jonson, that can surpass *The Revenger's Tragedy*. Tourneur excels in three virtues of the dramatist: he knew how, in his own way, to construct a plot, he was cunning in his manipulation of stage effects, and he was a master of versification and choice of language. *The Revenger's Tragedy* starts off at top speed, as every critic has observed; and never slackens to the end. We are told everything we need to know before the first scene is half over; Tourneur employs his torrent of words with the greatest economy. The opening scene, and the famous Scene v of Act III, are remarkable feats of melodrama; and the suddenness of the end of the final scene of Act V matches the sudden explosiveness of the beginning.

Before considering the detail of the two plays, we must face two problems which have never been solved and probably never will be: whether the two plays are by the same hand and, if so, in which order they were written. For the first point, the consensus of scholarship, with the exception of Mr. Oliphant's brilliant ascription of *The Revenger's Tragedy* to Middleton—an ascription which leaves the other play more of a mystery than before—assigns the two plays to Tourneur. For the second point, the consensus of scholarship is counter to the first impressions of sensibility; for all existing evidence points to the priority of *The Revenger's Tragedy* in time. The records of Stationers' Hall cannot be lightly disregarded; and Mr. Dugdale Sykes, who is perhaps our greatest authority on the texts of Tourneur and Middleton, finds stylistic evidence also. Professor Nicoll accepts the evidence, although pointing out clearly enough the anomaly. Certainly, any testimony drawn from the analogy of a modern poet's experience would urge that *The Atheist's Tragedy* was immature work, and that *The Revenger's Tragedy* represented a period of full mastery of blank verse. It is not merely that the latter play is in every way the better; but that it shows a highly original development of vocabulary and metric, unlike that of every other play and every other dramatist. The versification of *The Revenger's*

Tragedy is of a very high order indeed. And yet, with the evidence before us, summed up briefly in Mr. Nicoll's preface, we cannot affirm that this is the later play. Among all the curiosities of that curious period, when dramatic poets worked and developed in ways alien to the modern mind, this is one of the most curious. But it is quite possible. We may conjecture either that *The Atheist's Tragedy* was composed, or partly composed, and laid by until after *The Revenger's Tragedy* was written and entered. Or that after exhausting his best inspiration on the latter play—which certainly bears every internal evidence of having been written straight off in one sudden heat—Tourneur, years after, in colder blood, with more attention to successful models—not only Shakespeare but also perhaps Chapman—produced *The Atheist's Tragedy*, with more regular verse, more conventional moralizing, more conventional scenes, but with here and there flashes of the old fire. Not that the scenes of *The Atheist's Tragedy* are altogether conventional; or, at least, he trespasses beyond the convention in a personal way. There was nothing remarkable in setting a graveyard scene at midnight; but we feel that to set it for the action of a low assignation and an attempted rape at the same time seems more to be expected of the author of *The Revenger's Tragedy* than of anyone else; while the low comedy, more low than comic, does not seem of the taste of either Webster or Middleton. Webster's farcical prose is harmonious with his tragic verse; and in this respect Webster is a worthy follower of the tradition of the Porter in *Macbeth*. Middleton again, in his tragedies, has a different feel of the relation of the tragic and the comic; whereas the transitions in the two tragedies of Tourneur—and especially in *The Atheist's Tragedy*—are exactly what one would expect from a follower of Marston; especially in *The Atheist's Tragedy* they have that offensive tastelessness which is so positive as to be itself a kind of taste, which we find in the work of Marston.

The Atheist's Tragedy is indeed a peculiar brew of styles. It has well-known passages like the following:[1]

> *Walking next day upon the fatal shore,*
> *Among the slaughtered bodies of their men,*
> *Which the full-stomached sea had cast upon*
> *The sands, it was my unhappy chance to light*
> *Upon a face, whose favour when it lived*
> *My astonished mind informed me I had seen.*
> *He lay in his armour, as if that had been*

[1] The text used in the following quotations is the critical text of Professor Nicoll; but for convenience and familiarity the modernized spelling and punctuation of the 'Mermaid' text is used.

His coffin; and the weeping sea (like one
Whose milder temper doth lament the death
Of him whom in his rage he slew) runs up
The shore, embraces him, kisses his cheek;
Goes back again, and forces up the sands
To bury him, and every time it parts
Sheds tears upon him, till, at last (as if
It could no longer endure to see the man
Whom it had slain, yet loth to leave him) with
A kind of unresolved unwilling pace,
Winding her waves one in another, (like
A man that folds his arms, or wrings his hands
For grief) ebbed from the body, and descends;
As if it would sink down into the earth
And hide itself for shame of such a deed.

The present writer was once convinced that *The Atheist's Tragedy* was the earlier play. But lines like these, masterly but artificial, might well belong to a later period; the regularity of the versification, the elaboration of the long-suspended sentences, with three similes expressed in brackets, remind us even of Massinger. It is true that Charles Lamb, commenting on this passage, refers this parenthetical style to Sir Philip Sidney, who 'seems to have set the example to Shakespeare'; but these lines have closer syntactical parallels in Massinger than in Shakespeare. But lines like

To spend our substance on a minute's pleasure

remind one of *The Revenger's Tragedy,* and lines like

Your gravity becomes your perished soul
As hoary mouldiness does rotten fruit

of *The Revenger's Tragedy* where it is likest Middleton.

As a parallel for admitting the possibility of *The Atheist's Tragedy* being the later play, Professor Nicoll cites the fact that *Cymbeline* is later than *Hamlet.* This strikes us as about the most unsuitable parallel that could be found. Even though some critics may still consider *Cymbeline* as evidence of 'declining powers', it has no less a mastery of words than *Hamlet,* and possibly more; and, like every one of Shakespeare's plays, it adds something or develops something not explicit in any previous play; it has its place in an orderly sequence. Now accepting the canonical order of Tourneur's two plays, *The Atheist's Tragedy* adds nothing at all to what the other play has given us; there is no development, no fresh inspiration; only the skilful but uninspired use of a greater metrical variety. Cases are not altogether wanting, among poets, of a precocious maturity exceeding the limits of the poet's experience—in contrast to the very slow and very long development of Shakespeare—a maturity to which the poet is never again able to catch up. Tourneur's genius, in any case, is in *The Revenger's Tragedy*; his talent only in *The Atheist's Tragedy*.

Indeed, *The Revenger's Tragedy* might well be a specimen of such isolated masterpieces. It does express—and this, chiefly, is what gives it its amazing unity—an intense and unique and horrible vision of life; but is such a vision as might come, as the result of few or slender experiences, to a highly sensitive adolescent with a gift for words. We are apt to expect of youth only a fragmentary view of life; we incline to see youth as exaggerating the importance of its narrow experience and imagining the world as did Chicken Licken. But occasionally the intensity of the vision of its own ecstasies or horrors, combined with a mastery of word and rhythm, may give to a juvenile work a universality which is beyond the author's knowledge of life to give, and to which mature men and women can respond. Churton Collins's introduction to the works is by far the most penetrating interpretation of Tourneur that has been written; and this introduction, though Collins believed *The Revenger's Tragedy* to be the later play, and although he thinks of Tourneur as a man of mature experience, does not invalidate this theory. 'Tourneur's great defect as a dramatic poet,' says Collins, 'is undoubtedly the narrowness of his range of vision:' and this narrowness of range might

be that of a young man. The cynicism, the loathing
and disgust of humanity, expressed consummately
in *The Revenger's Tragedy*, are immature in the
respect that they exceed the object. Their objective
equivalents are characters practising the grossest
vices; characters which seem merely to be spectres
projected from the poet's inner world of nightmare,
some horror beyond words. So the play is a document on humanity chiefly because it is a document on one human being, Tourneur; its motive is
truly the death motive, for it is the loathing and
horror of life itself. To have realized this motive so
well is a triumph; for the hatred of life is an important phase—even, if you like, a mystical experience
—in life itself.

The Revenger's Tragedy, then, is in this respect
quite different from any play by any minor Elizabethan; it can, in this respect, be compared only to
Hamlet. Perhaps, however, its quality would be better marked by contrasting it with a later work of
cynicism and loathing, *Gulliver's Travels*. No two
compositions could be more dissimilar. Tourneur's
'suffering, cynicism and despair', to use Collins's
words, are static; they might be prior to experience,
or be the fruit of but little; Swift's is the progressive
cynicism of the mature and disappointed man of the
world. As an objective comment on the world,
Swift's is by far the more terrible. For Swift had

himself enough pettiness, as well as enough sin of pride, and lust of dominion, to be able to expose and condemn mankind by its universal pettiness and pride and vanity and ambition; and his poetry, as well as his prose, attests that he hated the very smell of the human animal. We may think as we read Swift, 'how loathesome human beings are'; in reading Tourneur we can only think, 'how terrible to loathe human beings so much as that'. For you cannot make humanity horrible merely by presenting human beings as consistent and monotonous maniacs of gluttony and lust.

Collins, we think, tended to read into the plays of Tourneur too much, or more than is necessary, of a lifetime's experience. Some of his phrases, however, are memorable and just. But what still remains to be praised, after Swinburne and Collins and Mr. Nicoll, is Tourneur's unique style in blank verse. His occasional verses are mediocre at best; he left no lyric verse at all; but it is hardly too much to say that, after Marlowe, Shakespeare and Webster, Tourneur is the most remarkable technical innovator—an innovator who found no imitators. The style of *The Revenger's Tragedy* is consistent throughout; there is little variation, but the rapidity escapes monotony.

Faith, if the truth were known, I was begot
After some gluttonous dinner; some stirring dish

Was my first father, when deep healths went round
And ladies' cheeks were painted red with wine,
Their tongues, as short and nimble as their heels,
Uttering words sweet and thick; and when they rose,
Were merrily disposed to fall again.
In such a whispering and withdrawing hour . . .
. . . and, in the morning
When they are up and drest, and their mask on,
Who can perceive this, save that eternal eye
That sees through flesh and all? Well, if anything be
damned,
It will be twelve o'clock at night. . . .

His verse hurries:

O think upon the pleasure of the palace!
Secured ease and state! the stirring meats,
Ready to move out of the dishes, that e'en now
Quicken when they are eaten!
Banquets abroad by torchlight! music! sports!
Bareheaded vassals, that had ne'er the fortune
To keep on their own hats, but let horns wear 'em!
Nine coaches waiting—hurry, hurry, hurry——

His phrases seem to contract the images in his effort
to say everything in the least possible space, the
shortest time

Age and bare bone
Are e'er allied in action . . .

To suffer wet damnation to run through 'em . . .
The poor benefit of a bewildering minute . . .

(*Bewildering* is the reading of the 'Mermaid' text;
both Churton Collins and Mr. Nicoll give *bewitch-
ing* without mentioning any alternative reading: it
is a pity if they be right, for *bewildering* is much the
richer word here.)

> *forgetful feasts . . .*
> *falsify highways . . .*

And the peculiar abruptness, the frequent change of
tempo, characteristic of *The Revenger's Tragedy*, is
nowhere better shown than by the closing lines:

This murder might have slept in tongueless brass,
But for ourselves, and the world died an ass.
Now I remember too, here was Piato
Brought forth a knavish sentence once;
No doubt (said he), but time
Will make the murderer bring forth himself.
'Tis well he died; he was a witch.
And now, my lord, since we are in for ever,
This work was ours, which else might have been
    slipped!
And if we list, we could have nobles clipped,
And go for less than beggars; but we hate
To bleed so cowardly, we have enough,
I'faith, we're well, our mother turned, our sister true,
We die after a nest of dukes. Adieu!

The versification, as indeed the whole style of *The Revenger's Tragedy*, is not that of the last period of the great drama. Although so peculiar, the metric of Tourneur is earlier in style than that of the later Shakespeare, or Fletcher, or Webster; to say nothing of Massinger, or Shirley, or Ford. It seems to derive, as much as from anyone's, from that of Marston. What gives Tourneur his place as a great poet is this one play, in which a horror of life, singular in his own or any age, finds exactly the right words and the right rhythms.

JOHN FORD

Among other possible classifications, we might divide the Elizabethan and Jacobean dramatists into those who would have been great even had Shakespeare never lived, those who are positive enough to have brought some positive contribution after Shakespeare, and those whose merit consists merely in having exploited successfully a few Shakespearian devices or echoed here and there the Shakespearian verse. In the first class would fall Marlowe, Jonson and Chapman; in the second, Middleton, Webster and Tourneur; in the third, Beaumont and Fletcher and Shirley as tragedian. This kind of division could not support very close question, especially in its distinction between the second and the third class; but it is of some use at the beginning, in helping us to assign a provisional place to John Ford.

The standard set by Shakespeare is that of a continuous development from first to last, a development in which the choice both of theme and of

dramatic and verse technique in each play seems to
be determined increasingly by Shakespeare's state of
feeling, by the particular stage of his emotional
maturity at the time. What is 'the whole man' is not
simply his greatest or maturest achievement, but the
whole pattern formed by the sequence of plays; so
that we may say confidently that the full meaning of
any one of his plays is not in itself alone, but in that
play in the order in which it was written, in its relation to all of Shakespeare's other plays, earlier and
later: we must know all of Shakespeare's work in
order to know any of it. No other dramatist of the
time approaches anywhere near to this perfection
of pattern, of pattern superficial and profound; but
the measure in which dramatists and poets approxi-
mate to this unity in a lifetime's work, is one of the
measures of major poetry and drama. We feel a
similar interest, in less degree, in the work of Jonson
and Chapman, and certainly in the unfinished work
of Marlowe; in less degree still, the interest is in the
work of Webster, baffling as the chronological
order of Webster's plays makes it. Even without an
œuvre, some dramatists can effect a satisfying unity
and significance of pattern in single plays, a unity
springing from the depth and coherence of a number of emotions and feelings, and not only from
dramatic and poetic skill. The *Maid's Tragedy*, or
A King and No King, is better constructed, and has

as many poetic lines, as *The Changeling*, but is far inferior in the degree of inner necessity in the feeling: something more profound and more complex than what is ordinarily called 'sincerity'.

It is significant that the first of Ford's important plays to be performed, so far as we have knowledge, is one which depends very patently upon some of the devices, and still more upon the feeling tone, of Shakespeare's last period. *The Lover's Melancholy* was licensed for the stage in 1628; it could hardly have been written but for *Cymbeline, The Winter's Tale, Pericles,* and *The Tempest.* Except for the comic passages, which are, as in all of Ford's plays, quite atrocious, it is a pleasant, dreamlike play without violence or exaggeration. As in other of his plays, there are verbal echoes of Shakespeare numerous enough; but what is more interesting is the use of the Recognition Scene, so important in Shakespeare's later plays, to the significance of which as a Shakespeare symbol Mr. Wilson Knight has drawn attention. In Shakespeare's plays, this is primarily the recognition of a long-lost daughter, secondarily of a wife; and we can hardly read the later plays attentively without admitting that the father-and-daughter theme was one of very deep symbolic value to him in his last productive years: Perdita, Marina and Miranda share some beauty of which his earlier heroines do not possess the secret. Now Ford is struck by the dramatic and poetic effectiveness of the situation, and uses it on a level hardly higher than that of the device of twins in comedy; so in *The Lover's Melancholy* he introduces two such scenes, one the recognition of Eroclea in the guise of Parthenophil by her lover Palador, the second her recognition (accompanied, as in *Pericles*, by soft music) by her aged father Meleander. Both of these scenes are very well carried out, and in the first we have a passage in that slow solemn rhythm which is Ford's distinct contribution to the blank verse of the period.

> *Minutes are numbered by the fall of sands,*
> *As by an hourglass; the span of time*
> *Doth waste us to our graves, and we look on it:*
> *An age of pleasure, revelled out, comes home*
> *At last, and ends in sorrow; but the life,*
> *Weary of riot, numbers every sand,*
> *Wailing in sighs, until the last drop down;*
> *So to conclude calamity in rest.*

The tone and movement are so positive that when in a dull masque by Ford and Dekker, called *The Sun's Darling*, we come across such a passage as

> *Winter at last draws on the Night of Age;*
> *Yet still a humour of some novel fancy*
> *Untasted or untried, puts off the minute*

JOHN FORD

Of resolution, which should bid farewell
To a vain world of weariness and sorrows. . . .

we can hardly doubt the identity of the author. The
scenes, as said above, are well planned and well
written, and are even moving; but it is in such scenes
as these that we are convinced of the incommensur-
ability of writers like Ford (and Beaumont and
Fletcher) with Shakespeare. It is not merely that they
fail where he succeeds; it is that they had no conception of what he was trying to do; they speak
another and cruder language. In their poetry there is
no symbolic value; theirs is good poetry and good
drama, but it is poetry and drama of the surface.
And in a play like *The Revenger's Tragedy,* or
Women Beware Women, or *The White Devil,* there is
some of that inner significance which becomes the
stronger and stronger undertone of Shakespeare's
plays to the end. You do not find that in Ford.

It is suggested, then, that a dramatic poet cannot
create characters of the greatest intensity of life unless his personages, in their reciprocal actions and
behaviour in their story, are somehow dramatizing,
but in no obvious form, an action or struggle for
harmony in the soul of the poet. In this sense Ford's
most famous, though not necessarily best play may
be called 'meaningless', and, in so far as we may be
justified in disliking its horrors, we are justified by

its lack of meaning. *'Tis Pity She's a Whore* is surely one of the most read of minor Jacobean plays, and the only one of Ford's which has been lately revived upon the stage. It is the best constructed, with the exception of *Perkin Warbeck*, and the latter play is somewhat lacking in action. To the use of incest between brother and sister for a tragic plot there should be no objection of principle: the test is, however, whether the dramatic poet is able to give universal significance to a perversion of nature which, unlike some other aberrations, is defended by no one. The fact that it is defended by no one might, indeed, lend some colour of inoffensiveness to its dramatic use. Certainly, it is to Ford's credit that, having chosen this subject—which was suggested by an Italian tale—he went in for it thoroughly. There is none of the prurient flirting with impropriety which makes Beaumont and Fletcher's *King and No King* meretricious, and which is most evident and nauseous in the worst play which Ford himself ever wrote, *The Fancies Chaste and Noble*; a kind of prurience from which the comedy of Wycherley is entirely free. Furthermore, Ford handles the theme with all the seriousness of which he is capable, and he can hardly be accused here of wanton sensationalism. It is not the sort of play which an age wholly corrupt would produce; and the signs of decay in Ford's age are more clearly visible in the plays of

Beaumont and Fletcher than in his own. Ford does
not make the unpleasant appear pleasant; and when,
at the moment of avowed love, he makes Annabella
say

> *Brother, even by our mother's dust, I charge you,*
> *Do not betray me to your mirth or hate . . .*

he is certainly double-stressing the horror, which
from that moment he will never allow you to forget; but if he did not stress the horror he would be
the more culpable. There is nothing in the play to
which could be applied the term appropriately used
in the advertisements of some films: the 'peppy
situation'.

We must admit, too, that the versification and
poetry, for example the fine speech of Annabella in
Act V, Sc. v., are of a very high order:

> *Brother, dear brother, know what I have been,*
> *And know that now there's but a dining-time*
> *'Twixt us and our confusion. . . .*
> *Be not deceived, my brother;*
> *This banquet is an harbinger of death*
> *To you and me; resolve yourself it is,*
> *And be prepared to welcome it.*

Finally, the low comedy, bad as it is, is more restrained in space, and more relevant to the plot, than
is usual with Ford; and the death of Bergetto ('is all

this mine own blood?') is almost pathetic. When all
is said, however, there are serious shortcomings to
render account of. The sub-plot of Hippolita is
tedious, and her death superfluous. More important,
the passion of Giovanni and Annabella is not shown
as an affinity of temperament due to identity of
blood; it hardly rises above the purely carnal infatuation. In *Antony and Cleopatra* (which is no more an
apology for adultery than *'Tis Pity* is an apology for
incest) we are made to feel convinced of an over-
powering attraction towards each other of two persons, not only in defiance of conventional morality,
and against self-interest: an attraction as fatal as that
indicated by the love-potion motif in *Tristran und
Isolde*. We see clearly why Antony and Cleopatra
find each other congenial, and we see their relation,
during the course of the play, become increasingly
serious. But Giovanni is merely selfish and self-
willed, of a temperament to want a thing the more
because it is forbidden; Annabella is pliant, vacillat-
ing and negative: the one almost a monster of ego-
tism, the other virtually a moral defective. Her rebel-
lious taunting of her violent husband has an effect
of naturalness and arouses some sympathy; but the
fact that Soranzo is himself a bad lot does not exten-
uate her willingness to ruin him. In short, the play
has not the general significance and emotional
depth (for the two go together) without which no

such action can be justified; and this defect separates it completely from the best plays of Webster, Middleton and Tourneur.

There are two other plays, however, which are superior to *'Tis Pity She's a Whore*. The first is *The Broken Heart*, in which, with *'Tis Pity* and *The Lover's Melancholy*, we find some of the best 'poetical' passages. Some of the best lines in *The Broken Heart* are given to the distraught Penthea; and, being reminded of another fine passage given to a crazed woman in *Venice Preserved*, we might be tempted to generalize, and suggest that it is easier for an inferior dramatic poet to write poetry when he has a lunatic character to speak it, because in such passages he is less tied down to relevance and ordinary sense. The quite irrelevant and apparently meaningless lines

> *Remember,*
> *When we last gathered roses in the garden,*
> *I found my wits; but truly you lost yours.*

are perhaps the purest poetry to be found in the whole of Ford's writings; but the longer and better known passage preceding them is also on a very high level:

> *Sure, if we were all Sirens, we should sing pitifully,*
> *And 'twere a comely music, when in parts*

One sung another's knell: the turtle sighs
When he hath lost his mate; and yet some say
He must be dead first: 'tis a fine deceit
To pass away in a dream; indeed, I've slept
With mine eyes open a great while. No falsehood
Equals a broken faith; there's not a hair
Sticks on my head but, like a leaden plummet,
It sinks me to the grave: I must creep thither;
The journey is not long.

Between the first and the second of these passages
there is, however, a difference of kind rather than
degree: the first is real poetry, the second is the echo
of a mood which other dramatic poets had caught
and realized with greater mastery. Yet it exhibits
that which gives Ford his most certain claim to perpetuity: the distinct personal rhythm in blank verse
which could be no one's but his alone.

As for the play itself, the plot is somewhat over-
loaded and distracted by the affairs of unfortunate
personages, all of whom have an equal claim on our
attention; Ford overstrains our pity and terror by
calling upon us to sympathize now with Penthea,
now with Calantha, now with Orgilus, now with
Ithocles; and the recipe by which good and evil are
mixed in the characters of Orgilus and Ithocles is
one which renders them less sympathetic, rather
than more human. The scene in which Calantha,

during the revels, is told successively the news of the death of her father, of Penthea and of her betrothed, and the scene in the temple which follows, must have been very effective on the stage; and the style is elevated and well sustained. The end of the play almost deserves the extravagant commendation of Charles Lamb; but to a later critic it appears rather as a recrudescence of the Senecan mood:

> *They are the silent griefs which cut the heart-strings,*
> *Let me die smiling.*

than as a profound searching of the human heart. The best of the play, and it is Ford at his best, is the character and the action of Penthea, the lady who, after having been betrothed to the man she loves, is taken from him and given to a rival to gratify the ambitions of her brother. Even here, Ford misses an opportunity, and lapses in taste, by making the un-loved husband, Bassanes, the vulgar jealous elderly husband of comedy: Penthea is a character which deserved, and indeed, required, a more dignified and interesting foil. We are also diverted from her woes by the selfish revengefulness of her lost lover, who, having been robbed of happiness himself, is determined to contrive that no one else shall be happy. Penthea, on the other hand, commands all our sympathy when she pleads the cause of her brother Ithocles, the brother who has ruined her life, with the Princess Calantha whom he loves. She is throughout a dignified, consistent and admirable figure; Penthea, and the Lady Katherine Gordon in *Perkin Warbeck*, are the most memorable of all Ford's characters.

Perkin Warbeck is little read, and does not contain any lines and passages such as those which remain in the memory after reading the other plays; but it is unquestionably Ford's highest achievement, and is one of the very best historical plays outside of the works of Shakespeare in the whole of Elizabethan and Jacobean drama. To make this base-born pretender to the throne of England into a dignified and heroic figure was no light task, and is not one which we should, after reading the other plays, have thought Ford competent to perform; but here for once there is no lapse of taste or judgment. Warbeck is made to appear as quite convinced that he is the lawful heir to the throne of England. We ourselves are left almost believing that he was; in the right state of uncertainty, wondering whether his kingly and steadfast behaviour is due to his royal blood, or merely due to his passionate conviction that he is of royal blood. What is more remarkable still, is that Ford has succeeded, not merely, as with Penthea, in creating one real person among shadows, but in fixing the right fitness and the right contrast between characters. Even at the end, when the earlier pretender, Lambert Simnel, who contentedly serves the King (Henry VII) in the humble capacity of falconer, is brought forward to plead with Perkin to accept a similar destiny, the scene is not degrading, but simply serves to emphasize the nobility and constancy of the hero. But to make a man, who went down to history as an impostor, into an heroic figure, was not Ford's only difficulty and success. The King of Scotland, in order to demonstrate his faith and emphasize his support of Perkin Warbeck's claim to the English throne, gives him to wife his own niece, the Lady Katherine Gordon, very much against her father's wishes. To make a lady, so abruptly given away to a stranger and dedicated to such very doubtful fortunes, into not only a loyal but a devoted wife, is not easy; but Ford succeeds. The introduction of her admirer, her countryman Lord Dalyell, does not disturb the effect, for Katherine is not shown as having already reciprocated his affection. Dalyell is merely present as a reminder of the kind of happy and suitable marriage which Katherine would have made in her own country, but for the appearance of Warbeck and the caprice of the King; and his touching devotion to her cause throughout the action only exhibits more beautifully her own devotion to her husband. Ford for once succeeded in a most difficult attempt; and the play of *Perkin Warbeck* is almost flawless.

Of Ford's other plays, *Love's Sacrifice* is reprinted in the 'Mermaid' selection. It has a few fine scenes, but is disfigured by all the faults of which Ford was capable. In the complete editions—the Moxon edition with introduction (to Ford and Massinger) by Hartley Coleridge is obtainable, and there is also the edition of the Quarto texts published at the University of Louvain, the first volume edited by the late Professor Bang, and the second (1927) by Professor De Vocht—there are no other plays solely by Ford which retain any interest. It is difficult now to assent to Lamb's words, 'Ford was of the first order of poets', or to Mr. Havelock Ellis's attempt (in his excellent introduction to the 'Mermaid' volume) to present Ford as a modern man and a psychologist. Mr. Ellis makes the assertion that Ford is nearer to Stendhal and Flaubert than he is to Shakespeare. Ford, nevertheless, depended upon Shakespeare; but it would be truer to say that Shakespeare is nearer to Stendhal and Flaubert than he is to Ford. There is a very important distinction to be drawn at this point. Stendhal and Flaubert, and to them might be added Balzac, are analysts of the individual soul as it is found in a particular phase of society; and in their work is found as much sociology as individual psychology. Indeed, the two are aspects of one thing; and the greater French novelists, from Stendhal to Proust, chronicle the rise, the regime, and the decay of the upper bourgeoisie in France. In Elizabethan and Jacobean drama, and even in the comedy of Congreve and Wycherley, there is almost no analysis of the particular society of the times, except in so far as it records the rise of the City families, and their ambition to ally themselves with needy peerages and to acquire country estates. Even that rise of the City, in *Eastward Hoe* and *Michaelmas Term*, is treated lightly as a foible of the age, and not as a symptom of social decay and change. It is indeed in the lack of this sense of a 'changing world', of corruptions and abuses peculiar to their own time, that the Elizabethan and Jacobean dramatists are blessed. We feel that they believed in their own age, in a way in which no nineteenth- or twentieth-century writer of the greatest seriousness has been able to believe in his age. And accepting their age, they were in a position to concentrate their attention, to their respective abilities, upon the common characteristics of humanity in all ages, rather than upon the differences. We can partly criticize their age through our study of them, but they did not so criticize it themselves. In the work of Shakespeare as a whole, there is to be read the profoundest, and indeed one of the most sombre studies of humanity that has ever been made in poetry; though it is in fact so comprehensive that we cannot qualify it as a whole as either glad or sorry. We recognize the same

assumption of permanence in his minor fellows.
Dante held it also, and the great Greek dramatists.
In periods of unsettlement and change we do not
observe this: it was a changing world which met the
eyes of Lucian or of Petronius. But in the kind of
analysis in which Shakespeare was supreme the other
Elizabethan and Jacobean dramatists differed only
in degree and in comprehensiveness.

Such observations are not made in order to cast
doubt upon the ultimate value or the permanence
of the greatest nineteenth-century fiction. But for
the age in which Shakespeare lived and the age into
which his influence extended after his death, it must
be his work, and his work as a whole, that is our
criterion. The whole of Shakespeare's work is *one*
poem; and it is the poetry of it in this sense, not the
poetry of isolated lines and passages or the poetry of
the single figures which he created, that matters
most. A man might, hypothetically, compose any
number of fine passages or even of whole poems
which would each give satisfaction, and yet not be
a great poet, unless we felt them to be united by one
significant, consistent, and developing personality.
Shakespeare is the one, among all his contemporaries, who fulfils these conditions; and the nearest to
him is Marlowe. Jonson and Chapman have the
consistency, but a far lower degree of significant
development; Middleton and Webster take a lower

place than these; the author of *The Revenger's Tragedy*, whether we call him Tourneur or Middleton or another, accomplishes all that can be accomplished within the limits of a single play. But in all these dramatists there is the essential, as well as the superficies, of poetry; they give the pattern, or we may say the undertone, of the personal emotion, the personal drama and struggle, which no biography, however full and intimate, could give us; which nothing can give us but our experience of the plays themselves. Ford, as well as Fletcher, wrote enough plays for us to see the absence of essential poetry. Ford's poetry, as well as Beaumont and Fletcher's, is of the surface: that is to say, it is the result of the stock of expressions of feeling accumulated by the greater men. It is the absence of purpose—if we may use the word 'purpose' for something more profound than any formulable purpose can be—in such dramatists as Ford, Beaumont, Fletcher, Shirley, and later Otway, and still later Shelley, which makes their drama tend towards mere sensationalism. Many reasons might be found, according to the particular historical aspect from which we consider the problem. But Ford, as dramatic poet, as writer of dramatic blank verse, has one quality which assures him of a higher place than even Beaumont and Fletcher; and that is a quality which any poet may envy him. The varieties of cadence and tone in blank verse are none too many, in the history of English verse; and Ford, though intermittently, was able to manipulate sequences of words in blank verse in a manner which is quite his own.

PHILIP MASSINGER

I

Massinger has been more fortunately and more fairly judged than several of his greater contemporaries. Three critics have done their best by him: the notes of Coleridge exemplify Coleridge's fine and fragmentary perceptions; the essay of Leslie Stephen is a piece of formidable destructive analysis; and the essay of Swinburne is Swinburne's criticism at its best. None of these, probably, has put Massinger finally and irrefutably into a place.

English criticism is inclined to argue or persuade rather than to state; and, instead of forcing the subject to expose himself, these critics have left in their work an undissolved residuum of their own good taste, which, however impeccable, is something that requires our faith. The principles which animate this taste remain unexplained. Canon Cruickshank's book[1] is a work of scholarship; and the advantage of good scholarship is that it presents us with evidence which is an invitation to the critical faculty of the reader: it bestows a method, rather than a judgment.

It is difficult—it is perhaps the supreme difficulty of criticism—to make the facts generalize themselves; but Mr. Cruickshank at least presents us with facts which are capable of generalization. This is a service of value; and it is therefore wholly a compliment to the author to say that his appendices are as valuable as the essay itself.

The sort of labour to which Mr. Cruickshank has devoted himself is one that professed critics ought more willingly to undertake. It is an important part of criticism, more important than any mere expression of opinion. To understand Elizabethan drama it is necessary to study a dozen playwrights at once, to dissect with all care the complex growth, to ponder collaboration to the utmost line. Reading Shakespeare and several of his contemporaries is pleasure enough, perhaps all the pleasure possible, for most. But if we wish to consummate and refine this pleasure by understanding it, to distil the last drop of it, to press and press the essence of each author, to apply exact measurement to our own sensations,

[1] *Philip Massinger.* By A. H. Cruickshank. Oxford: Blackwell. 1920.

then we must compare; and we cannot compare without parcelling the threads of authorship and influence. We must employ Mr. Cruickshank's judgments; and perhaps the most important judgment to which he has committed himself is this:

'Massinger, in his grasp of stagecraft, his flexible metre, his desire in the sphere of ethics to exploit both vice and virtue, is typical of an age which had much culture, but which, without being exactly corrupt, lacked moral fibre.'

Here, in fact, is our text: to elucidate this sentence would be to account for Massinger. We begin vaguely with good taste, by a recognition that Massinger is inferior: can we trace this inferiority, dissolve it, and have left any element of merit?

We turn first to the parallel quotations from Massinger and Shakespeare collocated by Mr. Cruickshank to make manifest Massinger's indebtedness. One of the surest of tests is the way in which a poet borrows. Immature poets imitate; mature poets steal; bad poets deface what they take, and good poets make it into something better, or at least something different. The good poet welds his theft into a whole of feeling which is unique, utterly different from that from which it was torn; the bad poet throws it into something which has no cohesion. A good poet will usually borrow from authors remote in time, or alien in language, or diverse in interest.

Chapman borrowed from Seneca; Shakespeare and Webster from Montaigne. The two great followers of Shakespeare, Webster and Tourneur, in their mature work do not borrow from him; he is too close to them to be of use to them in this way. Massinger, as Mr. Cruickshank shows, borrows from Shakespeare a good deal. Let us profit by some of the quotations with which he has provided us——

MASSINGER:

> *Can I call back yesterday, with all their aids*
> *That bow unto my sceptre? or restore*
> *My mind to that tranquillity and peace*
> *It then enjoyed?*

SHAKESPEARE:

> *Not poppy, nor mandragora,*
> *Nor all the drowsy syrops of the world*
> *Shall ever medicine thee to that sweet sleep*
> *Which thou owedst yesterday.*

Massinger's is a general rhetorical question, the language just and pure, but colourless. Shakespeare's has particular significance; and the adjective 'drowsy' and the verb 'medicine' infuse a precise vigour. This is, on Massinger's part, an echo, rather than an imitation or a plagiarism—the basest, because least conscious form of borrowing. 'Drowsy syrop' is a condensation of meaning frequent in Shakespeare, but rare in Massinger.

MASSINGER:

> *Thou didst not borrow of Vice her indirect,*
> *Crooked and abject means.*

SHAKESPEARE:

> *God knows, my son,*
> *By what by-paths and indirect crook'd ways*
> *I met this crown.*

Here, again, Massinger gives the general forensic statement, Shakespeare the particular image. 'Indirect crook'd' is forceful in Shakespeare; a mere pleonasm in Massinger. 'Crook'd ways' is a metaphor; Massinger's phrase only the ghost of a metaphor.

MASSINGER:

> *And now, in the evening,*
> *When thou should'st pass with honour to thy rest,*
> *Wilt thou fall like a meteor?*

SHAKESPEARE:

> *I shall fall*
> *Like a bright exhalation in the evening,*
> *And no man see me more.*

Here the lines of Massinger have their own beauty. Still, a 'bright exhalation' appears to the eye and makes us catch our breath in the evening; 'meteor' is a dim simile; the word is worn.

MASSINGER:

> *What you deliver to me shall be lock'd up*
> *In a strong cabinet, of which you yourself*
> *Shall keep the key.*

SHAKESPEARE:

> *'Tis in my memory locked,*
> *And you yourself shall keep the key of it.*

In the preceding passage Massinger had squeezed his simile to death, here he drags it round the city at his heels; and how swift Shakespeare's figure is! We may add two more passages, not given by our commentator; here the model is Webster. They occur on the same page, an artless confession.

> *Here he comes,*
> *His nose held up; he hath something in the wind,*

is hardly comparable to 'the Cardinal lifts up his nose like a foul porpoise before a storm', and when we come upon

> *as tann'd galley-slaves*
> *Pay such as do redeem them from the oar*

it is unnecessary to turn up the great lines in the *Duchess of Malfy*. Massinger fancied this galley-

slave; for he comes with his oar again in the
Bondman——

> *Never did galley-slave shake off his chains,*
> *Or looked on his redemption from the oar. . . .*

Now these are mature plays; and the *Roman Actor*
(from which we have drawn the two previous ex-
tracts) is said to have been the preferred play of its
author.

We may conclude directly from these quotations
that Massinger's feeling for language had out-
stripped his feeling for things; that his eye and his
vocabulary were not in co-operation. One of the
greatest distinctions of several of his elder contemporaries—we name Middleton, Webster, Tourneur
—is a gift for combining, for fusing into a single
phrase, two or more diverse impressions.

> *. . . in her strong toil of grace*

of Shakespeare is such a fusion; the metaphor identi-
fies itself with what suggests it; the resultant is one
and is unique——

> *Does the silk worm expend her yellow labours? . . .*
> *Why does yon fellow falsify highways*
> *And lays his life between the judge's lips*
> *To refine such a one? keeps horse and men*
> *To beat their valours for her?*

Let the common sewer take it from distinction. . . .
Lust and forgetfulness have been amongst us. . . .

These lines of Tourneur and of Middleton exhibit
that perpetual slight alteration of language, words
perpetually juxtaposed in new and sudden combina-
tions, meanings perpetually *eingeschachtelt* into meanings, which evidences a very high development of
the senses, a development of the English language
which we have perhaps never equalled. And, indeed, with the end of Chapman, Middleton, Webster, Tourneur, Donne, we end a period when the
intellect was immediately at the tips of the senses.
Sensation became word and word was sensation.
The next period is the period of Milton (though
still with a Marvell in it); and this period is initiated
by Massinger.

It is not that the word becomes less exact. Massinger is, in a wholly eulogistic sense, choice and
correct. And the decay of the senses is not inconsistent with a greater sophistication of language. But
every vital development in language is a development of feeling as well. The verse of Shakespeare
and the major Shakespearian dramatists is an innovation of this kind, a true mutation of species. The
verse practised by Massinger is a different verse from
that of his predecessors; but it is not a development
based on, or resulting from, a new way of feeling.

On the contrary, it seems to lead us away from feeling altogether.

We mean that Massinger must be placed as much at the beginning of one period as at the end of another. A certain Boyle, quoted by Mr. Cruickshank, says that Milton's blank verse owes much to the study of Massinger's.

'In the indefinable touches which make up the music of a verse [says Boyle], in the artistic distribution of pauses, and in the unerring choice and grouping of just those words which strike the ear as the perfection of harmony, there are, if we leave Cyril Tourneur's *Atheist's Tragedy* out of the question, only two masters in the drama, Shakespeare in his latest period and Massinger.'

This Boyle must have had a singular ear to have preferred Tourneur's secondary work to his *Revenger's Tragedy*, and one must think that he had never glanced at Ford. But though the appraisal be ludicrous, the praise is not undeserved. Mr. Cruickshank has given us an excellent example of Massinger's syntax——

> *What though my father*
> *Writ man before he was so, and confirm'd it,*
> *By numbering that day no part of his life*
> *In which he did not service to his country;*

Was he to be free therefore from the laws
And ceremonious form in your decrees?
Or else because he did as much as man
In those three memorable overthrows,
At Granson, Morat, Nancy, where his master,
The warlike Charalois, with whose misfortunes
I bear his name, lost treasure, men, and life,
To be excused from payment of those sums
Which (his own patrimony spent) his zeal
To serve his country forced him to take up?

It is impossible to deny the masterly construction of this passage; perhaps there is not one living poet who could do the like. It is impossible to deny the originality. The language is pure and correct, free from muddiness or turbidity. Massinger does not confuse metaphors, or heap them one upon another. He is lucid, though not easy. But if Massinger's age, 'without being exactly corrupt, lacks moral fibre', Massinger's verse, without being exactly corrupt, suffers from cerebral anæmia. To say that an involved style is necessarily a bad style would be preposterous. But such a style should follow the involutions of a mode of perceiving, registering, and digesting impressions which is also involved. It is to be feared that the feeling of Massinger is simple and overlaid with received ideas. Had Massinger had a nervous system as refined as that of Middleton, Tourneur, Webster, or Ford, his style would be a triumph. But such a nature was not at hand, and Massinger precedes, not another Shakespeare, but Milton.

Massinger is, in fact, at a further remove from Shakespeare than that other precursor of Milton—John Fletcher. Fletcher was above all an opportunist, in his verse, in his momentary effects, never quite a pastiche; in his structure ready to sacrifice everything to the single scene. To Fletcher, because he was more intelligent, less will be forgiven. Fletcher had a cunning guess at feelings, and betrayed them; Massinger was unconscious and innocent. As an artisan of the theatre he is not inferior to Fletcher, and his best tragedies have an honester unity than *Bonduca*. But the unity is superficial. In the *Roman Actor* the development of parts is out of all proportion to the central theme; in the *Unnatural Combat*, in spite of the deft handling of suspense and the quick shift from climax to a new suspense, the first part of the play is the hatred of Malefort for his son and the second part is his passion for his daughter. It is theatrical skill, not an artistic conscience arranging emotions, that holds the two parts together. In the *Duke of Milan* the appearance of Sforza at the Court of his conqueror only delays the action, or rather breaks the emotional rhythm. And we have named three of Massinger's best.

A dramatist who so skilfully welds together parts

which have no reason for being together, who fabricates plays so well knit and so remote from unity, we should expect to exhibit the same synthetic cunning in character. Mr. Cruickshank, Coleridge, and Leslie Stephen are pretty well agreed that Massinger is no master of characterization. You can, in fact, put together heterogeneous parts to form a lively play; but a character, to be living, must be conceived from some emotional unity. A character is not to be composed of scattered observations of human nature, but of parts which are felt together. Hence it is that although Massinger's failure to draw a moving character is no greater than his failure to make a whole play, and probably springs from the same defective sensitiveness, yet the failure in character is more conspicuous and more disastrous. A 'living' character is not necessarily 'true to life'. It is a person whom we can see and hear, whether he be true or false to human nature as we know it. What the creator of character needs is not so much knowledge of motives as keen sensibility; the dramatist need not understand people; but he must be exceptionally aware of them. This awareness was not given to Massinger. He inherits the traditions of conduct, female chastity, hymeneal sanctity, the fashion of honour, without either criticizing or informing them from his own experience. In the earlier drama these conventions are merely a framework, or an alloy necessary for working the metal; the metal itself consisted of unique emotions resulting inevitably from the circumstances, resulting or inhering as inevitably as the properties of a chemical compound. Middleton's heroine, for instance, in *The Changeling,* exclaims in the well-known words——

> *Why, 'tis impossible thou canst be so wicked,*
> *To shelter such a cunning cruelty*
> *To make his death the murderer of my honour!*

The word 'honour' in such a situation is out of date, but the emotion of Beatrice at that moment, given the conditions, is as permanent and substantial as anything in human nature. The emotion of Othello in Act V is the emotion of a man who discovers that the worst part of his own soul has been exploited by someone more clever than he; it is this emotion carried by the writer to a very high degree of intensity. Even in so late and so decayed a drama as that of Ford, the framework of emotions and morals of the time is only the vehicle for statements of feeling which are unique and imperishable: Ford's and Ford's only.

What may be considered corrupt or decadent in the morals of Massinger is not an alteration or diminution in morals; it is simply the disappearance of all the personal and real emotions which this morality supported and into which it introduced a kind of order. As soon as the emotions disappear the morality which ordered it appears hideous. Puritanism itself became repulsive only when it appeared as the survival of a restraint after the feelings which it restrained had gone. When Massinger's ladies resist temptation they do not appear to undergo any important emotion; they merely know what is expected of them; they manifest themselves to us as lubricious prudes. Any age has its conventions; and any age might appear absurd when its conventions get into the hands of a man like Massinger—a man, we mean, of so exceptionally superior a literary talent as Massinger's, and so paltry an imagination. The Elizabethan morality was an important convention; important because it was not consciously of one social class alone, because it provided a framework for emotions to which all classes could respond, and it hindered no feeling. It was not hypocritical, and it did not suppress; its dark corners are haunted by the ghost of Mary Fitton and perhaps greater. It is a subject which has not been sufficiently investigated. Fletcher and Massinger rendered it ridiculous; not by not believing it, but because they were men of great talents who could not vivify it; because they could not fit into it passionate, complete human characters.

The tragedy of Massinger is interesting chiefly according to the definition given before; the highest degree of verbal excellence compatible with the most rudimentary development of the senses. Massinger succeeds better in something which is not tragedy, in the romantic comedy. *A Very Woman* deserves all the praise that Swinburne, with his almost unerring gift of selection, has bestowed upon it. The probable collaboration of Fletcher had the happiest result; for certainly that admirable comic personage, the tipsy Borachia, is handled with more humour than we expect of Massinger. It is a play which would be enjoyable on the stage. The form, however, of romantic comedy is itself inferior and decadent. There is an inflexibility about the poetic drama which is by no means a matter of classical, or neoclassical, or pseudo-classical law. The poetic drama might develop forms highly different from those of Greece or England, India or Japan. Conceded the utmost freedom, the romantic drama would yet remain inferior. The poetic drama must have an emotional unity, let the emotion be whatever you like. It must have a dominant tone; and if this be strong enough, the most heterogeneous emotions may be made to reinforce it. The romantic comedy is a skilful concoction of inconsistent emotion, a *revue* of emotion. *A Very Woman* is surpassingly well plotted. The debility of romantic drama does not depend upon extravagant setting, or preposterous events, or inconceivable coincidences: all these might be found in a serious tragedy or comedy. It consists in an internal incoherence of feelings, a concatenation of emotions which signifies nothing.

From this type of play, so eloquent of emotional disorder, there was no swing back of the pendulum. Changes never come by a simple reinfusion into the form which the life has just left. The romantic drama was not a new form. Massinger dealt not with emotions so much as with the social abstractions of emotions, more generalized and therefore more quickly and easily interchangeable within the confines of a single action. He was not guided by direct communications through the nerves. Romantic drama tended, accordingly, toward what is sometimes called the 'typical', but which is not the truly typical; for the *typical* figure in a drama is always particularized—an individual. The tendency of the romantic drama was towards a form which continued it in removing its more conspicuous vices, was towards a more severe external order. This form was the Heroic Drama. We look into Dryden's 'Essay on Heroic Plays', and we find that 'love and valour ought to be the subject of an heroic poem'. Massinger, in his destruction of the old drama, had prepared the way for Dryden. The intellect had perhaps exhausted the old conventions. It was not able to supply the impoverishment of feeling.

Such are the reflections aroused by an examination of some of Massinger's plays in the light of Mr. Cruickshank's statement that Massinger's age 'had much more culture, but, without being exactly corrupt, lacked moral fibre'. The statement may be supported. In order to fit into our estimate of Massinger the two admirable comedies—*A New Way to Pay Old Debts* and *The City Madam*—a more extensive research would be required than is possible within our limits.

II

Massinger's tragedy may be summarized for the unprepared reader as being very dreary. It is dreary, unless one is prepared by a somewhat extensive knowledge of his livelier contemporaries to grasp without fatigue precisely the elements in it which are capable of giving pleasure; or unless one is incited by a curious interest in versification. In comedy, however, Massinger was one of the few masters in the language. He was a master in a comedy which is serious, even sombre; and in one aspect of it there are only two names to mention with his: those of Marlowe and Jonson. In comedy, as a matter of fact, a greater variety of methods were discovered and employed than in tragedy. The method of Kyd, as developed by Shakespeare, was the standard for

English tragedy down to Otway and to Shelley. But both individual temperament, and varying epochs, made more play with comedy. The comedy of Lyly is one thing; that of Shakespeare, followed by Beaumont and Fletcher, is another; and that of Middleton is a third. And Massinger, while he has his own comedy, is nearer to Marlowe and Jonson than to any of these.

Massinger was, in fact, as a comic writer, fortunate in the moment at which he wrote. His comedy is transitional; but it happens to be one of those transitions which contain some merit not anticipated by predecessors or refined upon by later writers. The comedy of Jonson is nearer to caricature; that of Middleton a more photographic delineation of low life. Massinger is nearer to Restoration comedy, and more like his contemporary, Shirley, in assuming a certain social level, certain distinctions of class, as a postulate of his comedy. This resemblance to later comedy is also the important point of difference between Massinger and earlier comedy. But Massinger's comedy differs just as widely from the comedy of manners proper; he is closer to that in his romantic drama—in *A Very Woman*—than in *A New Way to Pay Old Debts*; in his comedy his interest is not in the follies of love-making or the absurdities of social pretence, but in the unmasking of villainy. Just as the Old Comedy of Molière differs in principle from the new Comedy of Marivaux, so the Old Comedy of Massinger differs from the New Comedy of his contemporary Shirley. And as in France, so in England, the more farcical comedy was the more serious. Massinger's great comic rogues, Sir Giles Overreach and Luke Frugal, are members of the large English family which includes Barabas and Sir Epicure Mammon, and from which Sir Tunbelly Clumsy claims descent.

What distinguishes Massinger from Marlowe and Jonson is in the main an inferiority. The greatest comic characters of these two dramatists are slight work in comparison with Shakespeare's best—Falstaff has a third dimension and Epicure Mammon has only two. But this slightness is part of the nature of the art which Jonson practised, a smaller art than Shakespeare's. The inferiority of Massinger to Jonson is an inferiority, not of one type of art to another, but within Jonson's type. It is a simple deficiency. Marlowe's and Jonson's comedies were a view of life; they were, as great literature is, the transformation of a personality into a personal work of art, their lifetime's work, long or short. Massinger is not simply a smaller personality: his personality hardly exists. He did not, out of his own personality, build a world of art, as Shakespeare and Marlowe and Jonson built.

In the fine pages which Remy de Gourmont

devotes to Flaubert in his *Problème du Style*, the great critic declares:

'La vie est un dépouillement. Le but de l'activité propre de l'homme est de nettoyer sa personnalité, de la laver de toutes les souillures qu'y déposa l'éducation, de la dégager de toutes les empreintes qu'y laissèrent nos admirations adolescentes;'
and again:

'Flaubert incorporait toute sa sensibilité à ses œuvres. . . . Hors de ses livres, où il se transvasait goutte à goutte, jusqu'à la lie, Flaubert est fort peu intéressant.'
Of Shakespeare notably, of Jonson less, of Marlowe (and of Keats to the term of life allowed him), one can say that they *se transvasaient goutte à goutte*; and in England, which has produced a prodigious number of men of genius and comparatively few works of art, there are not many writers of whom one can say it. Certainly not of Massinger. A brilliant master of technique, he was not, in this profound sense, an artist. And so we come to inquire how, if this is so, he could have written two great comedies. We shall probably be obliged to conclude that a large part of their excellence is, in some way which should be defined, fortuitous; and that therefore they are, however remarkable, not works of perfect art.

This objection raised by Leslie Stephen to Massinger's method of revealing a villain has great

cogency; but I am inclined to believe that the cogency is due to a somewhat different reason from
that which Leslie Stephen assigns. His statement is
too *apriorist* to be quite trustworthy. There is no
reason why a comedy or a tragedy villain should not
declare himself, and in as long a period as the author
likes; but the sort of villain who may run on in this
way is a simple villain (simple not *simpliste*). Barabas
and Volpone can declare their character, because
they have no inside; appearance and reality are co-
incident; they are forces in particular directions.
Massinger's two villains are not simple. Giles Overreach is essentially a great force directed upon small
objects, a great force, a small mind; the terror of a
dozen parishes instead of the conqueror of a world.
The force is misapplied, attenuated, thwarted, by
the man's vulgarity: he is a great man of the City,
without fear, but with the most abject awe of the
aristocracy. He is accordingly not simple, but a
product of a certain civilization, and he is not
wholly conscious. His monologues are meant to be,
not what he thinks he is, but what he really is: and
yet they are not the truth about him, and he himself
certainly does not know the truth. To declare himself, therefore, is impossible.

Nay, when my ears are pierced with widows' cries,
And undone orphans wash with tears my threshold,

173

I only think what 'tis to have my daughter
Right honourable; and 'tis a powerful charm
Makes me insensible of remorse, or pity,
Or the least sting of conscience.

This is the wrong note. Elsewhere we have the right:

Thou art a fool;
In being out of office, I am out of danger;
Where, if I were a justice, besides the trouble,
I might or out of wilfulness, or error,
Run myself finely into a praemunire,
And so become a prey to the informer,
No, I'll have none of 't; 'tis enough I keep
Greedy at my devotion: so he serve
My purposes, let him hang, or damn, I care not . . .

And how well tuned, well modulated, here, the diction! The man is audible and visible. But from passages like the first we may be permitted to infer that Massinger was unconscious of trying to develop a different kind of character from any that Marlow or Jonson had invented.

Luke Frugal, in *The City Madam*, is not so great a character as Sir Giles Overreach. But Luke Frugal just misses being almost the greatest of all hypocrites. His humility in the first act of the play is more than half real. The error in his portraiture is not the extravagant hocus-pocus of supposed Indian necro-

mancers by which he is so easily duped, but the
premature disclosure of villainy in his temptation of
the two apprentices of his brother. But for this, he
would be a perfect chameleon of circumstance.
Here, again, we feel that Massinger was conscious
only of inventing a rascal of the old simpler farce
type. But the play is not a farce, in the sense in
which *The Jew of Malta, The Alchemist, Bartholomew
Fair* are farces. Massinger had not the personality to
create great farce, and he was too serious to invent
trivial farce. The ability to perform that slight distortion of *all* the elements in the world of a play or a
story, so that this world is complete in itself, which
was given to Marlowe and Jonson (and to Rabelais)
and which is pre-requisite to great farce, was denied
to Massinger. On the other hand, his temperament
was more closely related to theirs than to that of
Shirley or the Restoration wits. His two comedies
therefore occupy a place by themselves. His ways of
thinking and feeling isolate him from both the
Elizabethan and the later Caroline mind. He might
almost have been a great realist; he is killed by conventions which were suitable for the preceding literary generation, but not for his. Had Massinger been
a greater man, a man of more intellectual courage,
the current of English literature immediately after
him might have taken a different course. The defect
is precisely a defect of personality. He is not, how-

ever, the only man of letters who, at the moment
when a new view of life is wanted, has looked at life
through the eyes of his predecessors, and only at
manners through his own.

JOHN MARSTON

John Marston, the dramatist, has been dead for three hundred years. The date of his death, June 25th, 1634, is one of the few certain facts that we know about him; but the appearance of the first volume of a new edition of his works, as well as an edition of his best-known play by itself, is a more notable event than the arrival of his tercentenary[1]. For Marston has enjoyed less attention, from either scholars or critics, than any of his contemporaries of equal or greater rank; and for both scholars and critics he remains a territory of unexplored riches and risks. The position of most of his contemporaries is pretty well settled; one cannot go very far wrong in one's estimate of the dramatists with whom Marston worked;

[1] *The Plays of John Marston*, in three volumes. Edited by H. Harvey Wood. Volume I. (Edinburgh: Oliver and Boyd. 8s. 6d. net each.)

The Malcontent. Edited by G. B. Harrison. The Temple Dramatists. (Dent: 1s. 6d. net.)

but about Marston a wide divergency of opinion is still possible. His greater defects are such as anyone can see; his merits are still a matter for controversy.

Little has transpired of the events of Marston's life since Bullen presented in 1887 what has hitherto been the standard edition. The date and place of his birth have been unsettled; but the main facts—that his mother was Italian, that he was educated at Brasenose College and put to the law, that he wrote satires and then plays for a brief period and finally entered the Church—are undisputed. We are left with the unsupported statement of Ben Jonson that he beat Marston and took away his pistol; but, without necessarily impugning the veracity of Jonson, or suggesting that he wished to impress Drummond with his own superiority, having gone such a long journey to talk to him, we may do well to put aside the image of a mean and ridiculous figure which Jonson has left us before considering the value of Marston's work. And before reading the selections of Lamb, or the encomium of Swinburne, we should do better to read the plays of Marston—there are not many—straight through. Did Marston have anything of his own to say or not? Was he really a dramatist, or only a playwright through force of circumstances? And if he was a dramatist, in which of his plays was he at his best? In answering these questions we have, as with no other Elizabethan dramatist, the opportunity to go completely wrong; and that opportunity is an incentive.

Dr. Wood's first volume includes, besides *Antonio and Mellida* and *Antonio's Revenge*, *The Malcontent*. There are three quartos of *The Malcontent*: Dr. Wood tells us that he has followed the second (*B* in Dr. Greg's classification), but has adopted what seemed to him better and fuller readings from A and C. Dr. Harrison's text is, he tells us, the 'revised quarto', and he follows the Temple Dramatists principle (certainly the right one for such a series) of modernized spelling and punctuation. Our only complaint against both editors is that they have conscientiously limited themselves, in their notes, to what is verifiable, and have deprived themselves and their readers of that delight in aside and conjecture which the born annotator exploits. Dr. Harrison's glossary, for instance, omits some difficult words, but includes others of which the meaning is obvious; one wishes that editors of Elizabethan texts would take as their model that perfect annotator Mr. F. L. Lucas in his monumental edition of John Webster. Dr. Wood appears to have had the advantage of consulting Dr. Harrison's edition; and it must be said that they both refer the reader to Mr. Lucas's edition of Webster for fuller information on certain points. Both Dr. Wood and Dr. Harrison seem to be assured on one critical judgment: that

The Malcontent is the most important of Marston's plays. Dr. Harrison says forthright: '*The Malcontent* is Marston's best play.' Dr. Wood says only:

'The best of Marston's comedies and tragedies, and his great tragi-comedy, *The Malcontent*, have striking and original qualities. . . . *The Malcontent* is one of the most original plays of its period. . . .'
It is this assumption that we are privileged to examine.

If we read first the two plays with which collected editions, including Dr. Wood's, begin—*Antonio and Mellida* and *Antonio's Revenge*—our first impression is likely to be one of bewilderment, that anyone could write plays so bad and that plays so bad could be preserved and reprinted. Yet they are not plays that one wholly forgets; and the second reading, undertaken perhaps out of curiosity to know why such bad plays are remembered, may show that the problem is by no means simple. One at first suspects Marston to have been a poet, with no inclination to the stage, but driven thereto by need, and trying to write to the popular taste; just as a fastidious writer of to-day may produce, under financial pressure, something which he vainly imagines to be a potential best-seller. There is one immediate objection to this theory, even before we have read Marston's later work. It is that there is better *poetry* in these two plays, both in several passages, quotable and quoted, and in the general atmosphere, than there is in the *Satires*, *The Scourge of Villainy* or *Pygmalion*. The last of these was apparently an attempt to repeat the success of *Venus and Adonis*, and deserves only the fate of every piece of writing which is an attempt to do again what has already been done by a better man. The first are obviously lacking in personal conviction. The Satire, when all is said and done, is a form which the Elizabethans endeavoured to naturalize with very slight success; it is not until Oldham that a satire appears, sufficiently natural to be something more than a literary exercise. When Donne tries it, he is not any more successful than Marston; but Donne could write in no form without showing that he was a poet, and though his satires are not good satires, there is enough poetry in them, as in his epistles, to make them worth reading. Marston is very competent, and perfectly perfunctory. He wrote satires, as he wrote Pygmalion, in order to succeed; and when he found that the satire was more likely to lead him to the gaol than to success, he seems to have taken up, in the same spirit, the writing of plays. And however laboured the first two tragical plays may be, there is more poetry in them than in anything he had written before. So we cannot say that he was a 'poet', forced by necessity to become a 'dramatist'.

The second observation upon *Antonio and Mellida* and its sequel, if we may call 'sequel' a play of such different intent, is that their badness cannot be explained simply by incapacity, or even by plain carelessness. A blockhead could not have written them; a painstaking blockhead would have done better; and a careless master, or a careless dunce, would not have gone out of his way to produce the effects of nonsensicality which we meet. These two plays give the effect of work done by a man who was so exasperated by having to write in a form which he despised that he deliberately wrote worse than he could have written, in order to relieve his feelings. This may appear an over-ingenious apologetic; but it is difficult to explain, by any natural action of mediocrity, the absurd dialogue in Italian in which Antonio and Mellida suddenly express themselves in Act IV, Sc. i. The versification, such as it is, has for the most part no poetic merit; when it is most intelligible, as in the apostrophes of Andrugio, it is aiming at a conventional noble effect; but it has often, and more interestingly, a peculiar jerkiness and irritability, as of a writer who is, for some obscure reason, wrought to the pitch of exasperation. There are occasional reversions to an earlier vocabulary and movement, difficult to explain at the very end of the sixteenth century, reversions which to Ben Jonson must have seemed simple evidence of

technical incompetence. As in the Prologue to
Antonio's Revenge:

> *The rawish dank of clumsy winter ramps*
> *The fluent summer's vein; and drizzling sleet*
> *Chilleth the wan bleak cheek of the numb'd earth,*
> *While snarling gusts nibble the juiceless leaves*
> *From the nak'd shuddering branch. . . .*

or the line at the beginning of Act II:

> *The black jades of swart night trot foggy rings*
> *'Bout heaven's brow. . . .*

It is not only in passages such as these that we get the
impression of having to do with a personality which
is at least unusual and difficult to catalogue. Marston's minor comic characters, in these two plays,
are as completely lifeless as the major characters.
Whether decent or indecent, their drollery is as far
from mirth-provoking as can be: a continuous and
tedious rattle of dried peas. And yet something is conveyed, after a time, by the very emptiness and irrelevance of this empty and irrelevant gabble; there is
a kind of significant lifelessness in this shadow-show.
There is no more unarticulated scarecrow in the
whole of Elizabethan drama than Sir Jeffrey Balurdo. Yet Act V, Sc. i of *Antonio's Revenge* leaves
some impression upon the mind, though what it is
we may not be able to say.

'Ho, who's above there, ho? A murrain on all proverbs. They say hunger breaks through stone walls; but I am as gaunt as lean-ribbed famine, yet I can burst through no stone walls. O now, Sir Jeffrey, show thy valour, break prison and be hanged. Nor shall the darkest nook of hell contain the discontented Sir Balurdo's ghost. Well, I am out well; I have put off the prison to put on the rope. O poor shotten herring, what a pickle art thou in! O hunger, how thou domineer'st in my guts! O for a fat leg of ewe mutton in stewed broth, or drunken song to feed on! I could belch rarely, for I am all wind. O cold, cold, cold, cold, cold. O poor knight! O poor Sir Jeffrey, sing like an unicorn before thou dost dip thy horn in the water of death. O cold, O sing, O cold, O poor Sir Jeffrey, sing, sing!'

After this comes a highfalutin speech by Pandulpho, and cries of 'Vindicta!' Balurdo, like the others, is so unreal that to deny his reality is to lend him too much existence; yet we can say of the scene, as of the play, that however bad it is no one but Marston could have written it.

The peculiar quality, which we have not attempted to define, is less evident in most of the plays which follow, just because they are better plays. The most considerable—setting aside his work of collaboration—are *The Malcontent, The Dutch Cour-*

tesan, *The Insatiate Countess,* and *The Fawn.* Of
these, the last is a slight but pleasant handling of an
artificial situation, a kind of Courtship of Miles
Standish in which the princess woos the prince who
has come to sue on behalf of his father. The Insatiate
Countess is a poor rival of the White Devil; her
changes of caprice from lover to lover are rapid to
the point of farce; and when the Countess, brought
to the block for her sins, exclaims, in reply to the
executioner's bidding of 'Madam, put up your
hair':

> *O, these golden nets*
> *That have ensnared so many wanton youths,*
> *Not one but has been held a thread of life,*
> *And superstitiously depended on.*
> *Now to the block we must vail. What else?*

we may remark (if these lines are indeed Marston's)
that we have known this sort of thing done better
by another dramatist, and that it is not worth going
to Marston for what Webster can give us. *The
Dutch Courtesan* is a better play than either of these;
Freevill and Malheureux behave more naturally
than we expect of Marston's heroes; the Courtesan's
villainy is not incredible or unmotivated, and her
isolation is enhanced by her broken English; and the
heroine, Beatrice, has some charming verses to
speak and is not, according to the standards of that

stage and age, preposterously mild and patient. Yet the play as a whole is not particularly 'signed' by Marston; it is a theme which might have been handled as well, or better, by Dekker or Heywood. We are looking, not for plays of the same kind and in parts almost as good as those done by other dramatists. To prove that Marston is worth the attention of any but the Elizabethan scholar, we must convince the reader that Marston does something that no one else does at all: that there is a Marston tone, like the scent of a flower, which by its peculiarity sharpens our appreciation of the other dramatists as well as bringing appreciation of itself, as experiences of gardenia or zinnia refine our experience of rose or sweet-pea. With this purpose in mind, we may agree, with reservations, with the accepted view that *The Malcontent* is superior to any of the three other plays mentioned in the foregoing paragraph.

The superiority of *The Malcontent* does not lie altogether in more solid dramatic construction. The construction is hardly as close as that of *The Dutch Courtesan*, and the lighter passages have hardly the interest of under-plot which, in the other play, we find in the pranks played by Cocledemoy at the expense of Mulligrub. Marston at best is not a careful enough playwright to deserve comparison with his better-known contemporaries on this score. He can commit the grossest carelessness in confusing his own characters. Even in *The Malcontent* there appears to be one such lapse. Several of the earlier scenes seem to depend for their point upon Bianca being the wife of Bilioso (a sort of prototype of the Country Wife); but she is not so named in the list of characters, and the words of Ferneze to her in the last scene seem to indicate that Marston had forgotten this relationship.

Nor is the character of Malevole really comparable to that of Jacques. In the play of Shakespeare, Jacques is surrounded by characters who by their contrast with him, and sometimes by their explicit remarks, criticize the point of view which he expresses—a point of view which is indeed an almost consciously adopted humour. And while a malcontent drawn by Jonson lacks the depth and the variety which Shakespeare can give by human contrasts, he at least preserves a greater degree of consistency than does Malevole. The whole part is inadequately thought out; Malevole is either too important or not important enough. We may suppose that he has assumed his role primarily as a disguise, and in order to be present at his usurper's court on the easy footing of a tolerated eccentric. But he has the difficult role of being both the detached cynic and the rightful prince biding his time. He takes pity on Ferneze (himself not a very satisfying character, as after his pardon in Act IV he lets the play down badly in Act V, Sc. iii by his unseemly levity with Bianca). Yet Malevole, in his soliloquy in Act III, Sc. i, which is apparently not for the benefit of Bilioso but intended to express his true thoughts and feelings, alludes to himself as suffering from insomnia because he ' 'gainst his fate Repines and quarrels'—not a philosophical role, nor one to be expected of the magnanimous duke whom he has to be at the end. Whether his sarcasms are meant to be affected railing or savage satire, they fail of their effect.

Nor is any of the other characters very much alive. It is possible to find Dr. Harrison's praise of Maria, as a 'virtuous and constant wife who is alive and interesting', to be excessive, and to find even Maquerelle deficient in liveliness. The virtue of *The Malcontent*, indeed, resides rather in its freedom from the grosser faults to be expected of Marston than from any abundance of positive merits, when we hold it up to the standard, not of Shakespeare, but of the contemporaries of Shakespeare. It has no passages so moving as the confrontation of Beatrice and Franceschina in *The Dutch Courtesan*, and no comic element so sprightly as the harlequinades of Cocledemoy in the same play. It has, as critics have remarked, a more controlled and even diction. Swinburne does not elevate it to the position of Marston's best play; but he observes that 'the brooding anger, the resentful resignation, the impatient spirit of endurance, the bitter passion of disdain, which animate the utterance and direct the action of the hero, are something more than dramatically appropriate; it is as obvious that these are the mainsprings of the poet's own ambitions and dissatisfied intelligence, sullen in its reluctant submission and ardent in its implacable appeal, as that his earlier undramatic satires were the tumultuous and turbid ebullitions of a mood as morbid, as restless and as honest'.

We are aware, in short, with this as with Marston's other plays, that we have to do with a positive, powerful and unique personality. His is an original variation of that deep discontent and rebelliousness so frequent among the Elizabethan dramatists. He is, like some of the greatest of them, occupied in saying something else than appears in the literal actions and characters whom he manipulates.

It is possible that what distinguishes poetic drama from prosaic drama is a kind of doubleness in the action, as if it took place on two planes at once. In this it is different from allegory, in which the abstraction is something conceived, not something differently felt, and from symbolism (as in the plays of Maeterlinck) in which the tangible world is deliberately diminished—both symbolism and allegory be-

ing operations of the conscious planning mind. In
poetic drama a certain apparent irrelevance may be
the symptom of this doubleness; or the drama has
an under-pattern, less manifest than the theatrical
one. We sometimes feel, in following the words and
behaviour of some of the characters of Dostoevsky,
that they are living at once on the plane that we
know and on some other plane of reality from
which we are shut out: their behaviour does not
seem crazy, but rather in conformity with the laws
of some world that we cannot perceive. More fit-
fully, and with less power, this doubleness appears
here and there in the work of Chapman, especially
in the two *Bussy D'Ambois* plays. In the work of
genius of a lower order, such as that of the author of
The Revenger's Tragedy, the characters themselves
hardly attain this double reality; we are aware rather
of the author, operating perhaps not quite consciously through them, and making use of them to
express something of which he himself may not be
quite conscious.

It is not by writing quotable 'poetic' passages, but
by giving us the sense of something behind, more
real than any of his personages and their action, that
Marston establishes himself among the writers of
genius. There is one among his plays, not so far
mentioned, and not, apparently, widely read or
highly esteemed, which may be put forward with

the claim that it is his best, and that it is the most
nearly adequate expression of his distorted and ob-
structed genius: *The Wonder of Women,* otherwise
The Tragedy of Sophonisba. This is a fairly late play
in Marston's brief career, and we have reason to
guess that the author himself preferred it to his
others. As the 'tragedy which shall boldly abide the
most curious perusal', it gives the impression of being the play which Marston wrote most nearly to
please himself. Bullen found it 'not impressive', and
even Swinburne reserves his praise for a few scenes.
Yet the play has a good plot, is well constructed and
moves rapidly. There are no irrelevances and no
comic passages; it is austere and economical. The
rapidity with which the too-scheming Carthagin-
ians transfer their allegiance from Massinissa to
Syphax, his rival suitor for Sophonisba, bringing
about an alliance between Massinissa and Scipio, is
not unplausible, and keeps the reader in a state of
continuous excitement over the fortunes of war.
The scene in which the witch Erictho takes on the
form of Sophonisba in order to induce Syphax to lie
with her, is by no means what Bullen would have it,
a scene of gratuitous horror, introduced merely to
make our flesh creep; it is integral to the plot of the
play; and is one of those moments of a double
reality, in which Marston is saying something else,
which evidence his poetic genius. And the memor-

able passages are not, as in his earlier plays, plums
imbedded in suet; they may be taken as giving a
fair taste of the quality of the whole play—e.g.

> *though Heaven bears*
A face far from us, gods have most long ears;
Jove has a hundred marble marble hands.

Nothing in Nature is unserviceable,
No, not even inutility itself.
Is then for nought dishonesty in being?
And if it be sometimes of forced use,
Wherein more urgent than in saving nations?

Our vows, our faith, our oaths, why they're ourselves.

Gods naught foresee, but see, for to their eyes
Naught is to come or past; nor are you vile
Because the gods foresee; for gods, not we
See as things are; things are not as we see.

(This last quotation reminds us of Meredith's line,
'By their great memories the gods are known'; but
Marston has the better of it. Swinburne, in spite of
his ability to like almost any Elizabethan play that
can be tolerated, is less than fair, when he calls
Sophonisba 'laboured and ambitious', and speaks of
'jagged barbarisms and exotic monstrosities of metaphor'; and his derogatory quotation of the end of
Act II does injustice to a passage which is acceptable
enough in its context.)

> *I do not praise gods' goodness, but adore;*
> *Gods cannot fall, and for their constant goodness*
> *(Which is necessitated) they have a crown*
> *Of never-ending pleasures. . . .*

The following has a distinct originality:

> *Where statues and Jove's acts were vively limned*
> *Boys with black coals draw the veil'd parts of nature,*
> *And lecherous actions of imagin'd lust;*
> *Where tombs and beauteous urns of well-dead men*
> *Stood in assured rest, the shepherd now*
> *Unloads his belly, corruption most abhorr'd*
> *Mingling itself with their renowned ashes.*

The following has a fine Senecal ring:

> *My god's my arm; my life my heaven; my grave*
> *To me all end.*

And the last words of Sophonisba,

> *He that ne'er laughed may with a constant face*
> *Contemn Jove's frown: happiness makes us base.*

may be considered as a 'classical' comparison to the 'romantic' vein of Tourneur's

> *I think man's happiest when he forgets himself.*

It is hoped that the reader will see some justification for accumulating quotations from *Sophonisba*, and leaving the other plays unquoted. The quotations are intended to exhibit the exceptional consistency of texture of this play, and its difference of tone, not only from that of Marston's other plays, but from that of any other Elizabethan dramatist. In spite of the tumultuousness of the action, and the ferocity and horror of certain parts of the play, there is an underlying serenity; and as we familiarize ourselves with the play we perceive a pattern behind the pattern into which the characters deliberately involve themselves; the kind of pattern which we perceive in our own lives only at rare moments of inattention and detachment, drowsing in sunlight. It is the pattern drawn by what the ancient world called Fate; subtilized by Christianity into mazes of delicate theology; and reduced again by the modern world into crudities of psychological or economic necessity.

We may be asked to account, in giving this play such high place, for the fact that neither contemporary popularity nor the criticism of posterity yields any support. Well; it may be modestly suggested that in our judgments of Elizabethan plays in general we are very much influenced by Elizabethan standards. The fact that Shakespeare transcended all other poets and dramatists of the time imposes a Shakespearian standard: whatever is of the same kind of drama as Shakespeare's, whatever may be measured by Shakespeare, however inferior to Shakespeare's it may be, is assumed to be better than whatever is of a different kind. However catholic-minded we may be in general, the moment we enter the Elizabethan period we praise or condemn plays according to the usual Elizabethan criteria. Fulke Greville has never received quite his due; we approach Greville, and Daniel, with the assumption that they are 'not in the main current'. The minor poet who hitches his skiff astern of the great galleon has a better chance of survival than the minor poet who chooses to paddle by himself. Marston, in the one play on which he appears to have prided himself, is Senecal rather than Shakespearian. Had the great ship been that of a Corneille or a Racine, instead of a Shakespeare, Marston might cut a better figure now. He spent nearly the whole of his dramatic career writing a kind of drama against which we feel that he rebelled. In order to enjoy the one play which he seems to have written to please himself, we should read Greville and Daniel, of his affinity with whom he was probably quite unconscious, and we should come to him fresh from Corneille and Racine. He would, no doubt, have shocked the French dramatists by his improprieties, and the English classicists as well: nevertheless, he should be with them, rather than with the Shakespearians.